# The worse things get, the better we eat.

by Cathy Guisewite

Selected Cartoons from
MY GRANDDAUGHTER HAS FLEAS!

FAWCETT CREST • NEW YORK

A Fawcett Crest Book
Published by Ballantine Books


Library of Congress Catalog Card Number: 89-84809

ISBN 0-449-21917-8

This book comprises a portion of MY GRANDDAUGHTER HAS FLEAS! and is reprinted by arrangement with Andrews and McMeel, a Universal Press Syndicate Company.

Manufactured in the United States of America

First Ballantine Books Edition: May 1991

MY FRIENDS ALL HURRY HOME FROM WORK TO BE WITH THEIR HUSBANDS...THEY PLAN EVERY DAY AROUND SPENDING TIME WITH THEIR CHILDREN....

IT MAKES ME FEEL IT'S TIME TO MAKE SOME BIG CHANGES OF MY OWN, MOM. I THINK I'M FINALLY READY TO MAKE A REAL COMMITMENT.

OH, SWEETIE, YOU MEAN YOU'RE... YOU'RE... **YOU'RE**...
I'M GOING TO GET A DOG!

...MOM??
GO AWAY. I WANT TO BE ALONE WITH MY HAPPINESS.

CATHY, GETTING A DOG IS A HUGE RESPONSIBILITY.
I KNOW THAT, MOM.

HOW WILL YOU HAVE TIME TO FEED IT? HOW WILL YOU HAVE TIME TO TAKE IT OUTSIDE? HOW WILL YOU HAVE TIME TO TRAIN IT? HOW WILL YOU HAVE TIME TO TAKE IT TO THE VET? HOW WILL YOU HAVE TIME TO PLAY WITH IT?

DON'T WORRY, MOM!

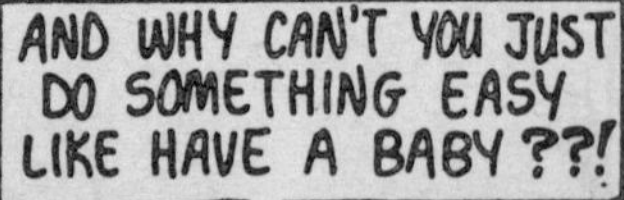
AND WHY CAN'T YOU JUST DO SOMETHING EASY LIKE HAVE A BABY??!

THE STAFF HERE AT THE HUMANE SOCIETY IS TRAINED TO BE ABLE TO TELL WHAT BREED OR BREEDS A PUPPY OR DOG MIGHT BE, AND WHAT HIS TEMPERAMENT AND SIZE WILL BE.
HUMANE SOCIETY
ADOPTION COUNSELOR

AFTER THAT, MOST PEOPLE JUST USUALLY GET A SPECIAL FEELING FROM ONE ANIMAL THAT LETS THEM KNOW IT'S THE RIGHT ONE FOR THEM TO ADOPT.
HUMANE SOCIETY

PICK ME.
PICK ME.
PICK ME.
PICK ME.
PICK ME.
PICK ME.
PICK ME.
PICK ME.
PICK ME.
PICK ME.
PICK ME.
PICK ME.
PICK ME.
PICK ME.

PLEASE
PLEASE.
PLEASE
PLEASE
PLEASE
PLEASE
PLEASE
PLEASE
PLEASE
PLEASE
PLEASE
PLEASE
PLEASE
PLEASE
I'M IN BIG TROUBLE.
HUMANE SOCIETY

WE HAVE DARLING PUPPIES, BEAUTIFUL MIXED BREEDS, AND LOVELY OLDER DOGS WHO ARE DESPERATE TO BE SOMEONE'S FRIEND.
I WILL MAKE A LOT OF MONEY AND BUY A HUGE HOUSE!
HUMANE SOCIETY

EVERY YEAR 7 MILLION DOGS AND CATS ARE PUT TO SLEEP BECAUSE PEOPLE DON'T GET THEIR PETS SPAYED OR NEUTERED.
I THOUGHT GETTING PETS FIXED MADE THEM FAT.
HUMANE SOCIETY

NOT TRUE. PETS ONLY GET FAT FOR THE SAME REASON PEOPLE GET FAT. DO YOU KNOW WHY PEOPLE GET FAT?

CERTAINLY. BECAUSE THEY INHERITED LOW METABOLISM AND A GENETIC ABUNDANCE OF FAT CELLS, COMBINED WITH A BIG BONE STRUCTURE, IN A SOCIO-ECONOMIC CLIMATE THAT ENCOURAGES THE CELEBRATION OF LIFE THROUGH CARBOHYDRATES!

THEY EAT TOO MUCH.
ALSO A POSSIBILITY.
HUMANE SOCIETY

LOTS OF PEOPLE THINK IT'S "MORE MASCULINE" FOR THEIR MALE PETS TO NOT GET FIXED, AND THAT FEMALE PETS "NEED THE MATERNAL EXPERIENCE."
HUMANE SOCIETY
Adopting A PET

BETWEEN THE "MACHO MALES" AND THE "MATERNAL EXPERIENCE," MORE THAN A MILLION NEW DOGS AND CATS WIND UP IN SHELTERS LIKE THIS EVERY MONTH WITH LITTLE HOPE OF EVER GETTING OUT.
HUMAN

IT COULD BE AVOIDED SO EASILY IF PEOPLE WOULD WAKE UP TO THE FACT THAT ANIMALS JUST DON'T THINK THE WAY WE DO.

I WANT MY MOTHER.

SHE'S LOOKING AT ME. DON'T ACT TOO EXCITED. SHE'LL THINK I'M HIGH-STRUNG.

DON'T ACT TOO CALM. SHE'LL THINK I'M BORING. JUST BE COOL. CON-FIDENT, YET CHARMING... COY, YET INTERESTED... JUST BE COOL.. EXUDE COOLNESS...RADIATE COOL...
HUMANE SOCIETY

MAY I SEE THIS ONE ?

WHAT DO YOU THINK ?
I SENSE THAT WE HAVE SOMETHING IN COMMON.
HUMANE SOCIETY

I CAN'T BELIEVE THAT PUPPY HASN'T BEEN TAKEN.
WELL, PEOPLE TEND TO TAKE ONLY THE CUTER DOGS. THIS ONE IS SO...
EXOTIC LOOKING.
HUMA SOCIE

SHE'LL MAKE A VERY NICE PET. SHE'S JUST SO.. YOU KNOW, SO...
PROFOUNDLY BEAUTIFUL.
HUMANE SOCIETY
ADOPTION COUNSELOR

I'M SURE YOU'LL GET ALONG FINE. COME TO THINK OF IT, YOU BOTH HAVE SORT OF THAT SAME....
CHOMP.
HUMANE SOCIETY
ADOPTION COUNSELOR

OW.
RAQUEL WELCH LOOK.
HUMANE SOCIETY
ADOPTION COUNSELOR

ANIMALS THAT HAVE BEEN ABANDONED ARE UNDERSTANDABLY NERVOUS ABOUT NEW PEOPLE.
ADOPTION COUNSELOR

YOU MAY WANT TO KEEP HER IN A NICE SECURE BOX UNTIL SHE GRADUALLY LEARNS TO START TRUSTING YOU AND HER NEW ENVIRONMENT.

OR YOU COULD JUST WEAR HER.

THIS IS THE BED WHERE YOU'LL SLEEP... THAT'S WHERE YOU'LL EAT... AND THERE'S THE LITTLE PLAY AREA WHERE YOU WILL KEEP ALL YOUR TOYS.

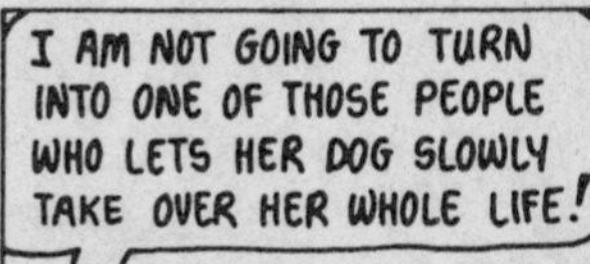
I AM NOT GOING TO TURN INTO ONE OF THOSE PEOPLE WHO LETS HER DOG SLOWLY TAKE OVER HER WHOLE LIFE!

IT'S SO MUCH MORE EFFICI-ENT TO JUST CAVE IN AFTER THE FIRST FIVE MINUTES.
CLICK

IT'S NORMAL FOR WOMEN CATHY'S AGE TO TRANSFER CERTAIN MATERNAL URGES ONTO A PET.

WE NEED TO ACT SUPPORTIVE OF HER DECISION TO GET A DOG, BUT ALSO REMIND HER THAT A DOG IS NO SUBSTITUTE FOR A REAL FAMILY. A DOG IS WONDERFUL, BUT IT'S JUST A DOG. A CANINE. AN ANIMAL. A PET.

COME TO GRAND-MA!!
MOM'S FINALLY FLIPPED.
I KNOW, CATHY.

...AND GRANDPA'S GOING TO GET SOME PICTURES OF IT!!

IRVING, MEET MY PUPPY, ELECTRA.
ELECTRA?? YOU NAMED HER WITHOUT EVEN ASKING MY OPINION??

I DIDN'T WANT ANYONE'S OPINION ON THIS, IRVING.

THERE COMES A TIME IN A WOMAN'S LIFE WHEN SHE NEEDS TO JUST LOOK INWARD FOR THE ANSWERS!
I TYPED OUT A BATCH OF 200 MORE NAME SUGGESTIONS, SWEETIE!

CAN I HELP IT IF EVERY TIME I LOOK INWARD, MY MOTHER IS STANDING THERE WITH A LIST?

"ELECTRA" MEANS "DAZZLING, BRIL-LIANT BEAUTY." IT'S THE PERFECT NAME FOR MY PUPPY!
CATHY, SHE'S JUST A BROWN, SCRAGGLY MUTT.

IRVING, DON'T SAY THAT IN FRONT OF HER.
DOGS DON'T UNDERSTAND WHAT WE'RE SAYING. HA, HA!

LOOK AT HER. SHE LOOKS LIKE A "SCRUFFY" OR A "MUFFY" OR A "TRAMP"....

HE LOOKS LIKE A GEEK.

LET ME SEE ALL THE OTHER NAMES YOU HAVE MARKED FOR THE PUPPY IN YOUR BABY NAME BOOK, CATHY.
BABY NAMES

OH...UM, THOSE WEREN'T FOR HER.
WHO WERE THEY FOR?
FOR?? AHEM...NO ONE..UM..
WHY WOULD YOU HAVE BA-BY NAMES MARKED? WHY WOULD YOU EVEN HAVE A BABY NAME BOOK???
BABY

OH, NEVER MIND THE BABY NAME BOOK, IRVING. I BOUGHT IT FOR CATHY AND I'LL PUT IT AWAY.
THANK YOU, MOM.
BABY NAMES

SHE KEEPS IT RIGHT HERE IN HER SECRET DRAWER NEXT TO HER FILE ON BRIDAL PARTY PLACE SETTINGS!!
BABY NAMES

DON'T GET UP EVERY TIME SHE MAKES A NOISE OR SHE'LL NEVER LEARN TO SLEEP THROUGH THE NIGHT, CATHY.

NEVER LET HER HAVE A SNACK UNTIL SHE'S FINISHED HER DINNER... NEVER LET HER GET AWAY WITH SOMETHING JUST BECAUSE SHE LOOKS CUTE...

PUPPIES ARE LIKE BABIES. THEY NEED A MOTHER WHO GIVES THEM RULES, DISCIPLINE AND CONSISTENTLY FIRM AUTHORITY...

...AND A GRANDMA WHO GIVES THEM ANYTHING THEY WANT !!

IRVING...UM, I'M TRYING TO TEACH ELECTRA TO NOT JUMP UP ON THE FURNITURE.
SHE WON'T HURT ANYTHING, CATHY.
COOKIES

I DON'T WANT HER TO BEG FOR FOOD.
IT'S JUST A LITTLE COOKIE.
SHE'S NOT SUPPOSED TO CHEW ON CLOTHING.
HA, HA! LOOK AT HER TUG!

IRVING, IT'S HARD ENOUGH FOR ME TO DISCIPLINE HER WITHOUT YOU HELPING HER BREAK EVERY RULE!
SHE'S JUST HAVING FUN, CATHY! HA, HA!

WHY MOTHERS CONTINUE TO GAIN WEIGHT AFTER THE BABY IS BORN.

NO, ELECTRA! BAD GIRL! YOU'RE SUPPOSED TO GO OUTSIDE! BAD BAD BAD!

OH, LOOK AT THAT FACE. DON'T LOOK SO SAD... HERE... HAVE SOME DOG BISCUITS... HAVE A COOKIE... EVERYONE MAKES MISTAKES....

CATHY, YOU'RE SCOLDING HER AND THEN STUFFING HER WITH FOOD TO EASE YOUR CONSCIENCE. I CAN'T BELIEVE MY EYES.

YOU'RE RAISING HER JUST THE WAY I RAISED YOU!!

Whine Yap Yap
OK, OK. I'LL MOVE YOUR BASKET TO THE BEDROOM, ELECTRA. JUST STOP WHIMPERING.

Whine Yap Yap
OK. YOU CAN SLEEP IN MY BED THIS ONCE. JUST BE QUIET.

Yap Yap Whine Whine
FINE. TAKE MY BED. TAKE MY BLANKETS. TAKE MY FOOD. JUST STOP MAKING THAT PATHETIC SOUND! I HAVE TO GET UP IN THREE HOURS!

SLEEP DEPRIVATION: THE FOUNDATION OF ALL GREAT OBEDIENCE PROGRAMS.
Z Z Z Z Z Z
COOKIES

SOME COUPLES DEAL WITH EVERY ISSUE THE SECOND IT COMES UP.

THAT HURT ME, DON.
LET'S TALK ABOUT IT, PAM.

SOME COUPLES LET LITTLE PROBLEMS ACCUMULATE UNTIL THEY MERIT A BIG DISCUSSION.

SOME THINGS ARE BOTHERING ME, KAREN.
WE'LL WORK THROUGH THEM TOGETHER, JOE.

SOME COUPLES NEVER ACTUALLY DEAL WITH THE INDIVIDUAL ISSUES, PREFERRING TO LET THEM KEEP HEAPING UP UNTIL THE FULL RANGE OF EMOTION CAN BE EXPRESSED.

THE "BURNING-THE-IN-BASKET" APPROACH TO PROBLEM-SOLVING.

YOU MAKE ME SICK!!!
PBLLLTTT!!!

"WHAT'S WRONG WITH YOU?"
"WHY CAN'T YOU COMMUNICATE?"
"WHEN ARE YOU GOING TO SHAPE UP?"

"THESE ARE ABSTRACT QUESTIONS THAT DO NOTHING TO IMPROVE A RELATIONSHIP."

"TO MAKE POSITIVE, HARMONIOUS CHANGES, PEOPLE MUST LEARN TO MAKE SPECIFIC COMMENTS THAT CAN BE ACTED UPON!"

WHY DON'T YOU THROW OUT THAT STUPID BOOK?
WHERE ARE ALL THE GOOD MEN?

A LOT OF COUPLES DON'T TALK ABOUT FEELINGS JUST BECAUSE THEY DREAD STARTING SOME LONG, EMOTIONAL CONFRONTATION, IRVING.

SO, THIS IS A TIMER. IF WE JUST SPEND FIVE MINUTES A WEEK DISCUSSING HOW WE FEEL, IMAGINE HOW WE COULD ENRICH OUR RELATIONSHIP!

WE MIGHT EVEN START LOOKING FORWARD TO IT.... FIVE LITTLE MINUTES A WEEK FOR US TO BE TOTALLY HONEST ABOUT EVERY HOPE, FEAR, ANXIETY, FRUSTRATION.....

BING!
TIME'S UP.
THANK HEAVENS.

TALKING ABOUT WHAT I WANT IN A RELATIONSHIP IS TORTURE FOR ME, CATHY.
YOU'RE SO DAR-LING...
OH. REALLY ? WELL, I MEAN, I CAN DO IT... I JUST.....
YOU'RE SO SMART. YOU'RE SO BRAVE. I LOVE YOU !!

IT'S NOT SO BAD ! LET'S TALK ! LET'S TALK ABOUT WHAT WE WANT !
YOU'RE SO PRECIOUS, ELECTRA ! HERE'S A NICE, BIG SNACK !

I WANT TO BE REINCAR-NATED AS A DOG.

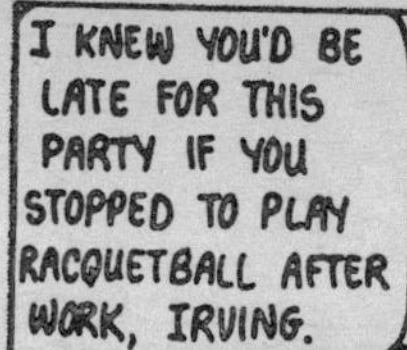

I KNEW YOU'D BE LATE FOR THIS PARTY IF YOU STOPPED TO PLAY RACQUETBALL AFTER WORK, IRVING.
THE SET JUST RAN LONG, CATHY.

I TOLD YOU YOU'D BE LATE.
OK. I WAS LATE.
I PREDICTED YOU'D BE LATE! I WAS SURE YOU'D BE LATE!
FINE. YOU WERE RIGHT.

I KNEW AT 9:00 THIS MORNING THAT YOU'D BE LATE TONIGHT!
FINE! YOU WERE RIGHT! YOU WIN!! NOW CAN WE DROP IT ?!!

IT ISN'T ENOUGH TO WIN. I WANT THE AWARDS CEREMONY.

YOU LOOK GREAT, CATHY!
GREAT?? HAH! THIS IS A DUMPY OLD SWEATSUIT! I LOOK LIKE AN EGGPLANT!

...NO. WAIT... THAT WAS HORRIBLE! I NOT ONLY POINTED OUT MY OWN FLAWS, BUT INSULTED YOUR JUDGMENT.

JUST START OVER, IRVING. COME IN AGAIN AND I'LL BE A MODEL OF POSITIVE SUPPORT!

YOU LOOK LIKE AN EGGPLANT.
I LOVE YOUR REPULSIVE SENSE OF HUMOR.

WAAHH!!
TURN THE CAR AROUND, LUKE.

WE CAN'T GO ON VACATION WITHOUT OUR BABY, LUKE!! WE'RE 35 MILES AWAY AND I CAN STILL HEAR HER SCREAMING! LUKE... PLEASE!

WAAHH!!

THAT'S YOUR VOICE, ANDREA.
OH.

IS LITTLE ZENITH STILL SHRIEKING AND SOBBING FOR HER MOMMY, CATHY ?
NO, ANDREA. SHE HASN'T CRIED AT ALL.
HONE

IS SHE THROWING TEMPER TANTRUMS ABOUT HER FOOD BECAUSE IT'S NOT HOW MOMMY MAKES IT ?
NO. SHE SEEMS PER-FECTLY HAPPY.
PHON

SHE'S PER-FECTLY HAPPY?
SHE'S HAVING A GREAT TIME, ANDREA! JUST RELAX AND ENJOY YOUR SPECIAL VACATION WITH YOUR HUSBAND!
PHON

DON'T TOUCH ME!!
PHONE

YOU'D BETTER BABY-PROOF THIS ROOM BEFORE YOU PUT ZENITH DOWN, CATHY.
I DON'T BELIEVE IN BABY-PROOFING, MOM.

A CHILD IS PERFECTLY ABLE TO RESPECT AN ADULT ENVIRONMENT IF YOU JUST TAKE A FEW MINUTES TO CLARIFY HER BOUNDARIES.

SMASH
RIP
WAD
BAM BAM
CHOMP
SPLAT
SHRED
TRAMPLE
STUFF
BOUNCE

ALL OF THAT WAS "NO."

ZENITH, PLEASE TAKE A NAP SO I CAN GET SOMETHING DONE! PLEASE... I HAVE TO FIX DINNER, DO THE LAUNDRY, CLEAN THE HOUSE, PAY BILLS...
EEYAA!

JUST TAKE A NAP! JUST GO TO SLEEP! I'M BEGGING YOU, ZENITH! TAKE A NAP! I CAN'T DO ANYTHING UNTIL YOU...
EEYAA!

EEEYAAA!
I MISSED IT!!

BA!
NO, ZENITH. YOUR MOMMY SAID NO TV UNTIL WE PRACTICE YOUR NUMBERS.

BA BA BA!
SEE THE FUNNY NUMBER BOOK? WON'T IT BE FUN TO LEARN ABOUT NUMBERS?

BA!

ZENITH: 483.
AUNT CATHY: ZILCH.

...OH, A BABY! LOOK! THEY HAVE A BABY!! WE HAVE A BABY, TOO!!
SCENIC POINT

WANT TO SEE PICTURES OF OUR BABY?? MAY I HOLD YOUR BABY?? LUKE, TAKE A PICTURE OF ME HOLDING THE BABY!!!

OH, I MISS OUR BABY!!
I ASSUME THIS IS YOUR FIRST?

OUR FIRST BABY, OR OUR FIRST VACATION AWAY FROM THE BABY?

CATHY SHOULD BE FINISHED GIVING ZENITH HER BATH AND BE CUDDLING UP FOR A LULLABY BEFORE PUTTING HER TO BED RIGHT NOW....

MARK MY WORDS, DEAR. THERE'S NOTHING LIKE CARING FOR SOMEONE ELSE'S SWEET LITTLE BABY TO MAKE A WOMAN'S OWN URGE FOR MOTHERHOOD KICK IN !!
RING, RING

RIP! BONK! SPLASH!
CLANK! MOM! BAM BAM!
SPLOOSH!

HER URGE FOR MOTHER KICKED IN.
IT'S A START...
Guisewite

THE BABY'S RUNNING THROUGH THE HOUSE NAKED, CATHY.
I'VE BEEN TRYING TO GET HER DRESSED AND IN BED FOR THREE HOURS, MOM.

I'M FRAZZLED! I'M CRACKING! I GIVE UP! I HAD NO IDEA ONE TINY HUMAN BEING COULD BE SO TOTALLY EXHAUSTING!!!

WHY AREN'T YOU SAYING ANYTHING?
SOMETIMES IT'S BEST FOR A MOTHER TO KEEP HER MOUTH CLOSED, SWEETIE.

IT KEEPS "I TOLD YOU SO" FROM JUMPING OUT.

LET'S SIT AND WATCH A MOVIE, ZENITH!
WAAAH!

OK. MOVIES ARE OUT. LET'S CALL A FRIEND.
WAAHH!!
FINE. CONVERSATIONS ARE OUT. LET'S DRIVE TO THE STORE.
WAAHH!!

I SEE. ALL ACTIVITIES LASTING MORE THAN THREE SECONDS ARE OUT FOR YOU.
Z

....EXCEPT FOR SMASHING A PAN WITH SPOONS, WHICH YOU CAN DO FOR AN HOUR AND A HALF STRAIGHT.
BAM BAM BAM
BAM BAM BAM BAM BAM BAM BAM BAM BAM BAM BAM BAM BAM BAM BAM

IS MY LITTLE ZENITH EATING HER ASPARAGUS-BASIL SOUP WITH OAT MUFFINS?
SHE'S EATING ANYTHING SHE WANTS, ANDREA.
PARK MAP
PHONE

IS SHE WEARING HER CUTE LITTLE RAW SILK ROMPER WITH MATCHING REEBOKS AND DOING HER NATURAL HISTORY MUSEUM FLASH CARDS?
SHE'S WEARING AND DOING ANYTHING SHE WANTS.

IS SHE TAKING HER BOYSENBERRY JUICE BOTTLE TO BED AND SNUGGLING RIGHT TO SLEEP AFTER ONE CD OF DULCIMER MOON SONGS??
SHE SLEEPS WHENEVER, HOWEVER, AND WHEREEVER SHE WANTS.

EVERYTHING'S UNDER AS MUCH CONTROL AS USUAL.
UH-OH.
PARK MAP
PHONE

ZENITH'S ANIMATED, INTERACTIVE, MICROCHIP-DRIVEN BEAR WITH VOICE, EYE, MOUTH AND PAW MOVEMENTS SYNCHRONIZED TO A SET OF VIDEOTAPE PRODUCTIONS OF "AESOP'S FABLES."

ZENITH'S HANDCRAFTED ITALIAN TEAK BUILDING-BLOCK SET WITH TINY FIGURES OF THE COMPLETE CAST OF THE "CIRQUE DU SOLEIL"... ... ZENITH'S ERGONOMICALLY CORRECT, MONO-FORK, FRONT-SUSPENSION TRICYCLE....

ZENITH'S NATURAL FIBER TYRANNOSAURUS PUPPET THAT SINGS THE FRENCH ALPHABET TO THE TUNE OF "OLD MAC DONALD"... ZENITH'S $300 LIBRARY OF POP-UP BOOKS FROM THE MUSEUM OF MODERN ART....

ZENITH'S FAVORITE TOY: AN EMPTY TOILET PAPER TUBE.

GA GA!
YOU'RE AMAZING, ZENITH.

YOU MAKE ME TOTALLY CRAZY ALL DAY... AND THEN, JUST AFTER I'VE HIT THE CRACKING POINT, YOU DO SOMETHING SO SWEET AND ENDEARING THAT I'D DO ANYTHING IN THE WORLD FOR YOU!

GA!

YOU REMIND ME OF MY BOYFRIEND.

FROM THE TIME WE'RE OLD ENOUGH TO SPEAK, WOMEN VOICE A CERTAIN COMPETITION ABOUT THE MEN IN OUR LIVES.

MY DADDY'S STRONGER THAN YOUR DADDY.
PBLTTT!

WITH EVERY YEAR, THE COMPARISONS ARE MORE INTENSE.
MY BOYFRIEND'S CUTER THAN YOUR BOYFRIEND.
PBLTTT!

UNTIL FINALLY--CONFIDENT OF OUR TASTES, SURE OF OUR NEEDS--WE REACH THE PINNACLE OF RIVALRY...THAT TRIUMPHANT, SELF-RIGHTEOUS MOMENT THAT MAYBE BEST DEFINES THE STATE OF AFFAIRS BETWEEN MEN AND WOMEN IN THE LATE 1980s....

THE RELATIONSHIP I DON'T HAVE IS BETTER THAN THE RELATIONSHIP YOU DON'T HAVE.
PBLTTT!

I THOUGHT YOU WEREN'T SEEING IRVING ANYMORE, CATHY.
I THOUGHT YOU WERE THROUGH WITH FRANKIE, CHARLENE.
LADIES

FRANKIE'S JUST MEETING ME FOR A FRIENDLY DRINK. IT'S NOT A DATE.
IRVING'S JUST STOPPING OVER TO DROP OFF SOME THINGS.

IT'S JUST FRIENDSHIP.
IT'S STRICTLY BUSINESS.
NO BIG DEAL.
A SIMPLE DELIVERY. TOTALLY MEANINGLESS.
SQUIRT
PUFF
DAB
FLUFF
POUF
POUF

DO I LOOK AS RIDICULOUS AS YOU LOOK?
ALMOST. YOU NEED SOME MORE LAVENDER ON THE LIDS.

ANY-THING I CAN DO, CATHY?
NO. I ORDERED DIN-NER AND DRINKS BY PHONE...MOVIES AND POPCORN ARE BEING DELIVERED LATER... AND I CALLED A MAID TO COME TOMORROW AND CLEAN UP.

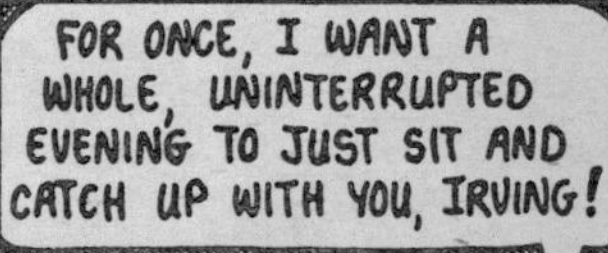
FOR ONCE, I WANT A WHOLE, UNINTERRUPTED EVENING TO JUST SIT AND CATCH UP WITH YOU, IRVING!

TO WHOM DO I SPEAK ABOUT HAVING SOME CONVERSATION SENT IN?

CHARLENE ?? I THOUGHT YOU WERE OUT WITH FRANKIE.
I'M CALLING FROM THE LADIES ROOM IN THE RESTAURANT, CATHY.

YOU HAVE TO LET FRANKIE AND ME COME OVER. WE'RE DYING HERE! WE NEED TO BE AROUND A FUN, LIVELY COUPLE!!
YOU WANT IRVING AND ME TO SAVE YOUR DATE??

I'M BEGGING YOU, CATHY! WHEN FRANKIE AND I AREN'T SCREAMING AT EACH OTHER ABOUT SOME PAST FIGHT, WE'RE JUST GLARING AT EACH OTHER IN SILENCE... PLEASE!!

WAKE UP, SWEETIE. THE ENTERTAINMENT IS ON THE WAY OVER.

FRANKIE, THIS IS CATHY'S FRIEND IRVING. IRVING IS ONE OF THE FUNNIEST MEN I EVER MET!

HE'S ALWAYS COMING UP WITH THESE GREAT ONE-LINERS! AND CATHY HAS ALL THESE HYSTERICAL STORIES!

GO AHEAD, YOU TWO! HA, HA! DON'T HOLD BACK!! LET THE WIT ROLL! LET THE HILARITY BEGIN!!

THEY'RE A RIOT, CHARLENE.
I KNEW YOU'D LOVE THEM.

HO, HUM... WE SHOULD BE GOING, CHARLENE.
I'M NOT READY TO GO YET, FRANKIE.

I HAVE TO GET UP EARLY FOR A MEETING. LET'S GO.
WHY DOES YOUR STUPID JOB ALWAYS DICTATE WHEN WE GO??!

MY STUPID JOB PAID FOR YOUR $27 BOWL OF SPAGHETTI!
IT WAS ANGEL HAIR PASTA AND YOU GRABBED THE CHECK!
GRABBED?? YOU WERE IN THE LADIES ROOM FOR 45 MINUTES!!
I ONLY PRIMP BECAUSE YOU'RE SO PICKY!!
HAH!
HAH!

WE'RE STAYING.
I HAVE TO GO.
YOU LIVE HERE, CATHY.
ARE THERE ANY REFRESHMENTS?

DID I TELL YOU ABOUT WHEN FRANKIE...
I AM NOT GOING TO SIT HERE WHILE YOU TELL THAT STUPID STORY FOR THE 400TH TIME, CHARLENE.

HOW DO YOU KNOW WHAT STORY I WAS GOING TO TELL?
I CAN TELL BY HOW YOUR NOSE WRIN-KLES UP!
I'D RATHER HAVE A NOSE THAT WRINKLES THAN A CHIN THAT WIGGLES!
MY CHIN IS NO WORSE THAN PARTS OF YOU I'M TOO POLITE TO MENTION!

I HATE IT WHEN YOU START AN ARGUMENT AND GET TOO SMUG TO FINISH IT!!
YOU DON'T KNOW HOW TO ARGUE!!
YOU MAKE ME CRAZY!
YOU MAKE ME SICK!!

CHARLENE, WHAT'S GOING ON WITH YOU TWO??
I DON'T KNOW. DO YOU THINK HE LIKES ME??

THE NEXT TIME YOU'RE HAVING A FIGHT WITH YOUR BOYFRIEND, DO NOT BRING HIM OVER HERE, CHARLENE.
OH, IT WASN'T THAT BAD, CATHY.

CHARLENE, YOU FILLED MY WHOLE HOUSE WITH THIS INCREDIBLE TENSION! WHAT DO YOU THINK IRVING AND I WILL DO NOW WHEN YOU LEAVE??

INVITE THEM BACK TOMORROW.
GUISEWITE

I'VE SPENT MY WHOLE LIFE OVERCOMING A POOR SELF-IMAGE.

I'VE WORKED, WORKED OUT, DIETED, STUDIED, SWEATED AND STRUGGLED TO DEVELOP A MIND, BODY AND CAREER I COULD FEEL GOOD ABOUT.

NOW--PROUD, ACCOMPLISHED AND TOTALLY SELF-ASSURED-- I WILL CURL UP WITH THE MAN I LOVE AND HEAR THE MOST INCREDIBLE WORDS OF MY LIFE...

YOUR LITTLE INSECURITIES ARE WHAT WILL ALWAYS MAKE YOU SO SPECIAL TO ME, CATHY.

WHY HAVEN'T YOU ASKED ABOUT IRVING, MOM?
I THOUGHT I WASN'T SUPPOSED TO ASK ABOUT IRVING ANYMORE.

NO. YOU WEREN'T SUPPOSED TO ASK ABOUT IRVING WHEN I WAS SEEING MITCH... YOU'RE NOT SUPPOSED TO ASK ABOUT MITCH ANYMORE... AND YOU'RE NEVER SUPPOSED TO ASK ABOUT ANYONE I'VE MENTIONED LESS THAN THREE TIMES OR MORE THAN SIX WEEKS AGO...

... BUT NOW I WANT YOU TO ASK ABOUT IRVING! I'VE BEEN HOPING YOU'D ASK!!

EVERY TIME I THINK I'M GETTING A GRIP ON THE JOB, SHE REVISES THE TRAINING MANUAL.

MY BILLS HAVE ALREADY ALL COME... THE JUNE BRIDES ARE ALL BACK FROM THEIR HONEYMOONS... ALL THE BABIES MY FRIENDS WERE EXPECTING HAVE BEEN BORN AND ANNOUNCED...

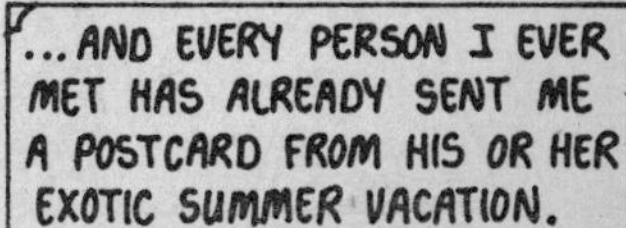
...AND EVERY PERSON I EVER MET HAS ALREADY SENT ME A POSTCARD FROM HIS OR HER EXOTIC SUMMER VACATION.

WE'RE HAVING AN AUGUST WEDDING!!

JUST WHEN I THOUGHT IT WAS SAFE TO GO BACK TO THE MAILBOX....
Guisewite

IF I TAKE IRVING TO THIS WEDDING, HE'LL THINK I'M TRYING TO SNEAK HIM INTO THE "WEDDING SPIRIT," WHICH WOULD BE TRUE.

IF I GO ALONE, PEOPLE WILL THINK I'M LOOKING TO MEET SOMEONE NEW, WHICH WOULD ALSO BE TRUE.

IF I DON'T GO AT ALL, IT WILL LOOK AS IF I'M PARA-NOID OR JEALOUS OR BOTH, ALL OF WHICH WOULD ALSO BE TRUE.

HOW LARGE OF A GIFT DO I HAVE TO BUY BEFORE I'M ABSOLVED OF ALL SUSPICION?

BRIDAL REGISTRY

MARLA, WHO "WAS NEVER INTO MATERIAL POSSESSIONS," HAS REGISTERED FOR $100-A-DINNER-PLATE CHINA.

ELAINE, WHO'S EATEN CARRY-OUT CHICKEN WITH A PLASTIC FORK FOR 15 YEARS, IS DOWN FOR $975 STERLING SILVER PLACE SETTINGS.

SHEILA, WHO DRINKS NOTHING BUT DIET COKE, HAS REQUESTED 24 CRYSTAL GOBLETS AT $125 A POP.

CATHY, WHO'S BROKE, IS DUMPING ALL REMAINING WOMEN FRIENDS WHO AREN'T ALREADY MARRIED.

WHAT'S YOUR WEDDING GOING TO BE LIKE, SHEILA?
LOOK! HERE'S MY DRESS! A LONG, BEAUTIFUL WHITE DRESS WITH A 6-FOOT TRAIN!

I'M GOING TO HAVE FLOWERS IN MY HAIR AND SATIN SHOES AND EVERYTHING IN THE ROOM IS DESIGNED TO MATCH! FIVE BRIDESMAIDS! FIVE USHERS! BOUQUETS ON EVERY PEW!!

I'M GOING TO LOOK LIKE A PRINCESS! OH, CATHY, FOR ONE WHOLE DAY I'LL FEEL JUST LIKE A PRINCESS!

I GUESS YOU OPTED FOR TRADITION.
I'M ONLY DOING IT FOR MY MOTHER.

MY FIANCE AND I ASKED OURSELVES, WHICH IS MORE IMPORTANT? A DOWN PAYMENT ON A HOUSE WE'LL OWN FOR 30 YEARS...OR A BEADED VEIL THAT WILL BE ON MY HEAD FOR 45 MINUTES?
BRIDE'S

A BRAND-NEW CAR... OR A SIX-TIER WEDDING CAKE WE'LL TAKE TWO BITES OF? A BASE OF FINANCIAL SECURITY... OR A 4-HOUR, $20,000 BASH?? WHAT WOULD YOU HAVE PICKED?
BRIDE'S

THE VEIL, THE CAKE AND THE BASH!
OH, CATHY, IT'LL BE THE HAPPIEST DAY OF OUR LIVES!
BRIDE'S

...THE LAST ONE WE'RE NEVER IN DEBT.
BRIDE'S

WHAT IF MY BRIDESMAIDS DON'T FIT INTO THEIR GOWNS?? WHAT IF THE ORCHIDS DON'T MATCH THE CUMMERBUNDS??

WHAT IF THE CATERER FORGETS THE POACHED SALMON?? WHAT IF THE VIDEO CREW DOESN'T GET ALL THE SHOTS??

SHEILA, RELAX. ONLY ONE THING REALLY MATTERS ON THE BIG DAY.
WHAT IF THEY MIS-SPELL OUR NAMES ON THE COCKTAIL NAPKINS?!!

ARE YOU NERVOUS ABOUT YOUR WEDDING TOO, PHIL?
WHAT IF SHE STAYS LIKE THIS AFTER WE'RE MARRIED?

WHY DON'T YOU WANT TO GO TO THIS WEDDING WITH ME, IRVING?

BECAUSE WHEN A MAN GOES TO A WEDDING WITH A WOMAN, IT MAKES HER START THINKING ABOUT A WEDDING WITH HIM.
IRVING, GOING TO A WEDDING WITH YOU IS NOT GOING TO MAKE ME START THINKING ABOUT A WEDDING WITH YOU!!

REALLY?
DON'T BE RIDICULOUS.

I HAD OUR WEDDING PLANNED AND OUR CHILDREN'S NAMES PICKED OUT 15 MINUTES AFTER WE MET.

TEN YEARS AGO I WOULD NOT HAVE CHANGED MY NAME IF I GOT MARRIED, BUT NOW IT DOESN'T SEEM SO BAD.... I PLEDGED TO NEVER QUIT MY JOB IF I HAD CHILDREN, BUT NOW I'M SORT OF LOOKING FORWARD TO A SABBATICAL....

TEN YEARS OF REVOLUTION, AND SUDDENLY I'M WILLINGLY GIVING UP MY NAME, MY CAREER PATH AND EVERY PRIORITY I THOUGHT I HAD.
MODERN BRIDE

SET ONE FOOT IN MY BATHROOM, AND YOU'RE A DEAD MAN, SWEETHEART!!!

SOME POINTS WILL NEVER BE NEGOTIABLE.
THE SPIRIT LIVES, SHEILA.
YOUR WEDDING

I THOUGHT YOU WERE DEAD SET AGAINST GOING TO THIS WEDDING WITH ME, IRVING.
I WAS... BUT THEN I THOUGHT ABOUT HOW IMPORTANT IT IS TO YOU, CATHY.

REALLY? YOU'RE JUST DOING IT TO MAKE ME HAPPY??
OF COURSE. I'D DO ANYTHING TO MAKE YOU HAPPY.

YOU KNOW WHY I'D DO ANYTHING TO MAKE YOU HAPPY, DON'T YOU, BEAUTIFUL?
YES...

BASEBALL PLAYOFF SEASON IS ONLY A MONTH AWAY.

SHEILA, THE WEDDING WAS JUST BEAUTIFUL. I...
CONGRATULATIONS SHEILA & PHIL

SHE'S MARRIED! SHE FINALLY GOT MARRIED! OH, HAPPY DAY!! OH, THANK THE HEAVENS!!

OH, KISS THE GROUND! IT'S A MIRACLE!! SHE'S MARRIED!! SHE FINALLY GOT MARRIED!!

I THINK YOUR MOTHER HAS SUMMED IT UP FOR ALL OF US.
Guisewite

WHAT A WEDDING! THEY MET ONLY 10 MONTHS AGO, BUT THEY JUST KNEW IT WAS RIGHT!
YES. HOW NICE.
CONGRATUL

MY HUSBAND PROPOSED ON OUR THIRD DATE. WE JUST KNEW IT WAS RIGHT, TOO! WHEN IT'S RIGHT, YOU JUST KNOW IT, DON'T YOU THINK?
HA, HA. YES. HOW LOVELY.
CONGRATUL

AND HOW LONG HAVE YOU TWO BEEN DATING??
NONE OF YOUR BUSINESS!

MORE THAN FIVE YEARS. I CAN TELL BY HOW HER EYES BUGGED OUT.
STAY AWAY FROM THE PUNCH, MOTHER.

HI. I'M RALPH. UNCLE OF THE BRIDE.... AND YOU MUST BE CATHY AND IRVING, THE SINGLE PEOPLE! HA, HA! WHEN ARE YOU TWO TYING THE KNOT??

HI! MAYBE YOU KIDS WILL BE NEXT! HA, HA!
DO WE HEAR WEDDING BELLS IN THE FUTURE??

NOTHING LIKE A WEDDING DAY TO POP THE QUESTION!
YOU'D MAKE SUCH A LOVELY BRIDE!
YOU DON'T KNOW HAPPINESS TILL YOU'VE WALKED DOWN THE AISLE!

...SIGH... TO BE SINGLE AGAIN....

I HAD TO CRY AT THE WEDDING BECAUSE IT WAS SO WONDERFUL TO SEE TWO PEOPLE SO MUCH IN LOVE... THEN I CRIED BECAUSE MAYBE I'LL NEVER HAVE THAT....

THEN I CRIED WHEN I MET ALL THE WEIRD RELATIVES BECAUSE I MIGHT TURN INTO ONE. ...THEN I CRIED BECAUSE I WAS SO RELIEVED YOU WERE THERE... THEN I CRIED BECAUSE YOU WERE SEEING ME WITH MASCARA ALL OVER MY FACE...

I DON'T KNOW HOW I'M SUPPOSED TO RESPOND, CATHY.

IF YOU HAVE ANYTHING HORRIBLE TO SAY TO ME, DO IT NOW WHILE I HAVE SOME MOMENTUM.

5:31.... THE OFFICE IS EMPTY. HOW CAN THE OFFICE BE EMPTY??
IN
IN

LOOK AT ALL THIS WORK! LOOK AT ALL THESE MESSES! LOOK AT ALL THESE EMERGENCIES!!

WHERE IS EVERYONE?? COME BACK HERE, EVERYONE!! COME BACK HERE AND HELP ME DO ALL THIS WORK!!

SOMETIMES I FEEL LIKE A FLY THAT GOT TRAPPED INSIDE AFTER THE PICNIC WAS CARRIED OUT.

TED! WHERE HAVE YOU BEEN?!
I JUST CAME IN TO PACK UP. MY WIFE AND I ARE LEAVING THE STRESS BEHIND AND OPENING A "BED AND BREAKFAST" IN OJAI, CALIF.

BOB AND I ARE LEAVING THE STRESS AND PROVIDING A TOX-IN-FREE ENVIRONMENT FOR OUR CHILDREN BY REINVENTING OUR-SELVES AS FREE-RANGE CHICK-EN FARMERS IN MONTANA!

MY FAMILY AND I ARE SELLING THE CONDO AND MOVING TO A TEPEE IN NEW MEXICO, WHERE WE'LL NOT ONLY PURGE OUR-SELVES OF URBAN STRESS AND TOXINS, BUT EXIST WITH NO CON-TACT WHATSOEVER WITH 1988!

WHAT'S THIS??
THE NEW GENERATION OF OVERACHIEVER QUITTERS.

YOU'RE QUITTING, TED?? JUST LIKE THAT??
EVERYONE'S STARTING TO RETHINK PRIORITIES, CATHY.

WE'VE GIVEN ALL WE HAD TO OUR CAREERS... SACRIFICED EVENINGS, WEEKENDS, RELATIONSHIPS, HEALTH....

I MEAN, AFTER 15 YEARS OF KILLING YOURSELF FOR A JOB, YOU HAVE TO STOP AND ASK YOURSELF SOME PRETTY MAJOR QUESTIONS.

WHERE'S ALL THE MONEY??

EVERYONE USED TO COME BACK FROM VACATION TAN AND READY TO WORK...THIS YEAR, EVERYONE'S COMING BACK PALE AND READY TO QUIT.
IN

WE'RE TIRED OF FEELING BURNED-OUT, CATHY. SICK OF GETTING FRIED. WE'VE LEARNED THE DANGERS OF TOO MUCH HEAT.
IN

SO YOU'RE GIVING UP YOUR WHOLE CAREER??
I'M NOT GIVING UP MY WHOLE CAREER.
FWOMP!
IN

I'M JUST LOOKING FOR A JOB WITH A HIGHER SUN-SCREEN FACTOR.

MR. PINKLEY, I...
OH, THANK HEAVENS IT'S YOU, CATHY! YOU WOULDN'T BELIEVE THE PEOPLE WHO'VE PARADED IN HERE TODAY DEMANDING RAISES!!
THEY THINK THAT JUST BECAUSE 10 PEOPLE QUIT, THERE ARE 10 SALARIES TO PASS AROUND!!

YOU'RE THE ONE PERSON I KNEW WHO'D HAVE AN ASTUTE ENOUGH GRASP OF THE BIG PICTURE TO NOT TURN OUR CORPORATE CRISIS INTO A QUEST FOR PERSONAL GAIN!!
$5,000 OR I WALK, MR. PINKLEY.

NEXT.

MR. PINKLEY, IN A NORMAL COMPANY, WHEN 10 PEOPLE QUIT, THEY HIRE 10 NEW PEOPLE TO REPLACE THEM.

SOME COMPANIES MIGHT HIRE ONLY FIVE NEW PEOPLE, BUT GIVE HUGE RAISES TO THOSE WHO'D BE DOING ALL THE WORK OF THE FIVE THEY DIDN'T REPLACE.

BUT NO COMPANY ON EARTH WOULD LET 10 PEOPLE LEAVE, HIRE NO REPLACEMENTS, AND EXPECT THE MEASLY REMAINING STAFF TO DO ALL THE WORK WITH NO EXTRA MONEY!!

AT LAST! WE'VE FOUND OUR UNIQUE NICHE!!

ELECTRA, MY PUPPY, IS WAITING FOR ME AT HOME. WHAT A WONDERFUL FEELING!

SHE'S THERE...WAITING JUST FOR ME! FOR THE FIRST TIME IN MY LIFE, I FINALLY UNDERSTAND WHAT MY FRIENDS HAVE BEEN SAYING ABOUT THEIR CHILDREN ALL THESE YEARS....

AACK!
ARF!

THEY ALWAYS NEED A HUG JUST WHEN YOU NEED TO SCREAM AT THEM.

WHAT A DAY.
I'M EXHAUSTED.
I CAN'T MOVE.

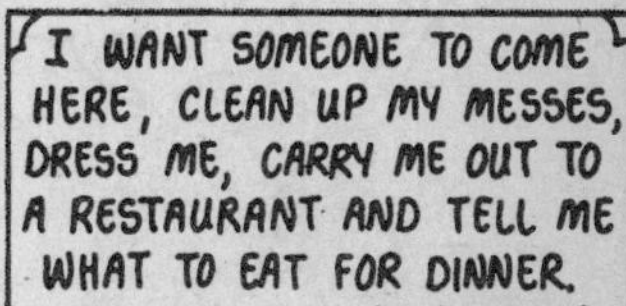
I WANT SOMEONE TO COME HERE, CLEAN UP MY MESSES, DRESS ME, CARRY ME OUT TO A RESTAURANT AND TELL ME WHAT TO EAT FOR DINNER.

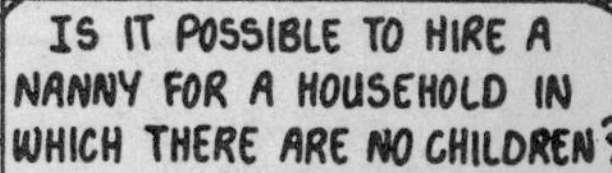
IS IT POSSIBLE TO HIRE A NANNY FOR A HOUSEHOLD IN WHICH THERE ARE NO CHILDREN?

YOU'VE HAD A HARD WEEK. WHY DON'T I BRING SOME DINNER OVER?
THANKS, IRVING, BUT I'M NOT EXACTLY FIXED UP FOR COMPANY...

CATHY, I'VE SEEN YOU "NOT FIXED UP" A HUNDRED TIMES. YOU LOOK GREAT!

I LOVE IT WHEN YOU'RE JUST COMPLETELY NATURAL! I'LL BE RIGHT OVER.
OK... BUT YOU'RE GOING TO SEE THE REAL ME...

...A WOMAN WHO CAN DO A COMPLETE MAKE-OVER IN SIX MINUTES.

HERE, CATHY. NOTHING HELPS GET RID OF STRESS LIKE A MASSAGE.
HE'S FEELING HOW FAT MY SHOULDERS ARE...

TENSIONS EVAPORATE... WORRIES DISAPPEAR...
HE'S SQUASHING THE FAT ON MY BACK...HE'S GOING TO KNEAD THE FAT ON MY WAIST AND THEN ...THEN....

ENOUGH! THANK YOU!! WHEW! THANK YOU! GREAT MASSAGE!!

I HARDLY EVEN STARTED.
THIS IS AS RELAXED AS I CAN STAND TO GET.

THE WHOLE FINKEL CRISIS FELL IN MY LAP TODAY, IRVING!
DID YOU GET IT DONE?

YES. BUT IT WAS CHAOS! A NIGHTMARE!
BUT YOU GOT IT DONE. THAT'S GREAT!

IRVING, IT WAS HORRIBLE! DOWN TO THE WIRE! HEART ATTACK CITY!!
CATHY, YOU MADE IT. YOU'RE HERE. ONLY ONE THING'S IMPORTANT NOW.

FORCING YOU TO LISTEN TO A MINUTE-BY-MINUTE REPLAY.

Yap Yap Yap
ELECTRA, IT'S 3:00 IN THE MORNING... I CAN'T TAKE YOU OUT NOW.

Yap Yap Yap
IT'S DARK AND FREEZING OUT-SIDE. I'M TOO SLEEPY. I CAN'T GET UP.

YAP YAP YAP
LEAVE ME ALONE! JUST GO ON THE FLOOR! I'LL CLEAN IT UP TOMORROW!!

I DON'T THINK I'M READY TO BE A MOTHER.

"IF YOUR PUPPY IS NOT HOUSE-BROKEN AFTER TWO MONTHS OF TRYING, YOU ARE FAILING TO BE CLEAR ABOUT YOUR WISHES."

"AS IN ALL OTHER KINDS OF TRAINING, HOUSEBREAKING CAN HAPPEN ONLY WHEN YOU GIVE FIRM, EXACTING GUIDELINES FOR WHAT IS ACCEPTABLE."

"MANY PET OWNERS NOTICE DRAMATIC IMPROVEMENT BY INCORPORATING ONE SIMPLE KEY PHRASE INTO THE TRAINING COMMAND STRUCTURE."

HOW'S YOUR PUPPY, ELECTRA, CATHY?
OH, SHE'S SO CUTE! SHE SLEEPS WITH HER HEAD RIGHT ON THE PILLOW NEXT TO MINE!
COFFEE ROOM RULES

MY CAT DOES THE SAME THING. SHE JUST SORT OF NUZZLES ME TO WAKE ME UP!
WHEN I WAKE UP, ELECTRA HAS HER ARM AROUND MY NECK AS IF SHE'S BEEN HUGGING ME ALL NIGHT!

SIGH.

REMEMBER WHEN WE USED TO TALK ABOUT MEN THIS WAY?
DON'T GET ME STARTED, CHARLENE...

AACK! THOSE ARE MY NEW SUEDE PUMPS! YOU'RE EATING MY NEW SUEDE PUMPS!!

ELECTRA, A WOMAN'S SHOES ARE SACRED! A WOMAN'S SHOES ARE HER LIFE! YOU ARE NEVER, NEVER, NEVER TO GET YOUR POINTY LITTLE TEETH NEAR A PAIR OF WOMAN'S SHOES!!!

BOOTS!

"PUNISHING A DOG AFTER THE FACT IS CONFUSING AND FRUSTRATING FOR THE ANIMAL."
Puppy Training

"THE WORD 'NO' IS ONLY EFFECTIVE IF YOU SAY IT AT THE VERY MOMENT YOUR PUPPY IS DOING SOMETHING WRONG."
Puppy Training

"ONCE YOUR PUPPY KNOWS THE REPERCUSSIONS OF BEING CAUGHT IN THE ACT, SHE WILL QUICKLY LEARN THE KEY TO HAVING A HARMONIOUS LIFE WITH YOU."
Puppy Training

SPEED.
Puppy Training

EVEN WHEN MY BABY IS 20 MILES AWAY WITH A BABY SITTER ALL DAY, I KNOW EXACTLY WHAT SHE'S DOING.
ME, TOO.

MY LITTLE NICOLE IS HAVING HER JUICE BOTTLE RIGHT NOW!
MY LITTLE JACOB IS JUST WAKING UP FROM HIS NAP!

MY LITTLE MEGAN IS ALL CURLED UP WATCHING HER "E.T." TAPE!
MY LITTLE NOAH IS PLAYING WITH HIS RED TRUCK!

MY LITTLE PUPPY IS DOING SOMETHING REALLY HIDEOUS INVOLVING THE LIVING ROOM CARPET.

YOU DIDN'T HAVE ANY TROUBLE HOUSEBREAKING YOUR PUPPY, DID YOU, CATHY?
ME? OH, WELL, I...
COFF ROOM

OUR LITTLE SNUGGLES WAS HOUSEBROKEN THE SECOND DAY!
ELECTRA LEARNED QUICKLY, TOO!
WE CORRECTED HER ONCE AND THEN SHE JUST KNEW!
ELECTRA KNEW WITHOUT ME EVER TELLING HER!

WE CAN LEAVE HER FOR HOURS AND SHE'D NEVER MAKE A MISTAKE!!
ELECTRA NOT ONLY WAITS ALL DAY, BUT INSISTS THAT I TAKE A NICE HOT SHOWER AFTER WORK BEFOR TAKING HER OUT! HAH!!
COFFE ROOM

CROSS MELINDA OFF THE LIST OF PEOPLE WHO WILL EVER BE ALLOWED NEAR MY LIVING ROOM CARPET.

"REWARDING YOUR PUPPY WITH TREATS WILL ONLY LEAD TO OBESITY AND BEGGING."

"INSTEAD, PRAISE YOUR PUPPY WITH A LITTLE PAT AND WARM WORD.... AND YOU WILL SEE THE HAPPY GLOW OF A PUPPY FULL OF PRIDE AND LOVE FOR HER OWNER."
TRAIN YOUR PUPPY

GOOD GIRL, ELECTRA!

WHERE'S THE FOOD?

I THINK I'LL GO SEE HOW CATHY'S DOING WITH LITTLE ELECTRA.
CATHY WILL SCREAM IF YOU BRING HER ANY MORE CLIP-PINGS ON HOW TO HOUSEBREAK A PUPPY.

I'M NOT BRINGING ANY HOUSE-BREAKING CLIPPINGS.
SHE DOESN'T WANT ANY MORE SPEECHES. NO TIPS. NO HINTS. NO LECTURES.

BELIEVE ME, DEAR. I UNDER-STAND THE SENSITIVITIES OF GROWN CHILDREN WITH LITTLE ONES OF THEIR OWN!!

THEY'LL TURN AWAY A MOTHER FULL OF ADVICE, BUT THEY'LL NEVER SAY NO TO ONE HOLDING A MOP.

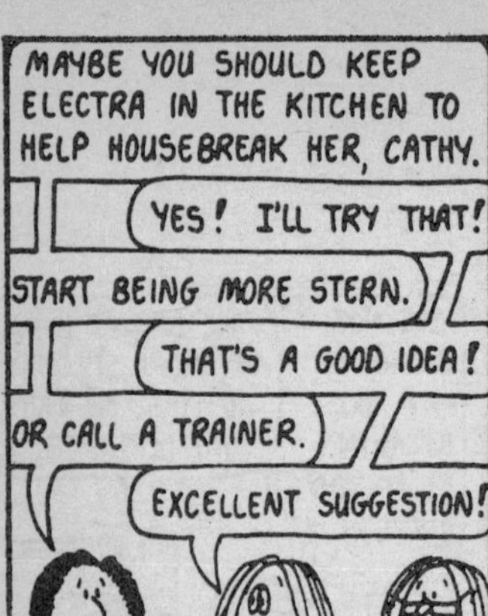
MAYBE YOU SHOULD KEEP ELECTRA IN THE KITCHEN TO HELP HOUSEBREAK HER, CATHY.
YES! I'LL TRY THAT!
START BEING MORE STERN.
THAT'S A GOOD IDEA!
OR CALL A TRAINER.
EXCELLENT SUGGESTION!

I DO NOT NEED YOUR OPINIONS, MOTHER! I KNOW WHAT I'M DOING! I HAVE EVERYTHING UNDER CONTROL!!

YOU MAY RULE HER HEART, BUT YOU WILL NEVER CONTROL HER BRAIN.

ELECTRA, I'M PUTTING THIS NEWSPAPER ON THE FLOOR IN CASE I CAN'T COME HOME AT LUNCH TO TAKE YOU OUT.

CATHY, DO YOU ACTUALLY THINK SHE UNDERSTANDS WHY YOU PUT NEWSPAPER ON THE FLOOR ??
SHE'S VERY SMART, IRVING.

OF COURSE SHE UNDERSTANDS WHY I PUT NEWSPAPER ON THE FLOOR!

SO I CAN READ SNOOPY.
Guisewite

I THOUGHT YOU WERE TEACHING ELECTRA NOT TO JUMP, CATHY.
I AM. SHE'S NOT ALLOWED TO JUMP IF I'M WEARING A DRESS, SUIT OR NATURAL-FIBER SKIRT.

ALL DARK PANTS ARE "NO JUMPING" EXCEPT MY TWO OLDEST BLUE JEANS, UNLESS I'M WEARING THEM WITH MY SUEDE BOOTS, WHICH COULD BE SCRATCHED.

SHE CAN JUMP ON THE PINK COTTON SWEATER, THE TAN PULL-OVER, AND ANY OF THE SWEAT-SHIRTS EXCEPT, OF COURSE, THE LAVENDER "TON-SUR-TON"!

WHEN PEOPLE WONDER WHAT DOGS THINK ABOUT ALL DAY, THEY FORGET HOW MUCH MEMORIZATION IS INVOLVED.

EXCELLENT JOB, CATHY!
UH-OH.

YOUR PERFORMANCE HAS BEEN BRILLIANT!
ANY TIME YOU COMPLIMENT ME I KNOW YOU'RE ABOUT TO MAKE ME DO SOMETHING HORRIBLE, MR. PINKLEY.

YOU'RE SHARP! TENACIOUS! DILIGENT! DYNAMIC!!
IT MUST BE REALLY HIDEOUS! A HIDEOUS NIGHTMARE ASSIGNMENT!

AND HAVE I MENTIONED WHAT REMARKABLE INTUITION YOU HAVE??
AACK.

I KNOW YOU WON'T MAKE ME GO GROVELING TO A CLIENT THAT YOU INFURIATED, MR. PINKLEY.
I KNOW YOU WON'T LET ME DOWN WHEN I REALLY NEED YOU, CATHY.

I KNOW YOU WON'T HUMILIATE ME JUST TO SAVE YOUR OWN PRIDE!
I KNOW YOU WON'T FORGET ALL THE TIMES I'VE BEEN THERE FOR YOU!

AFTER EVERYTHING WE'VE BEEN THROUGH TOGETHER, I KNOW YOU WON'T DO THIS TO ME!!!

THE STAND-OFF IS OVER, BUT THE GUILT-OFF HAS JUST BEGUN.
CHARLENE

WHY CAN'T JAN GO ON THIS BUSINESS TRIP? I HAVE A NEW PUPPY TO TAKE CARE OF.
JAN HAS FOUR CHIL-DREN.
PINKLEY

WHY CAN'T RICK GO? I HAVE A CRISIS WITH MY BOYFRIEND I HAVE TO RESOLVE.
RICK'S IN THE MIDDLE OF A DIVORCE.
PINKLEY

WHY CAN'T BOB GO? I HAVE 10 OTHER CLIENT EMERGEN-CIES TO DEAL WITH!
BOB HAS SIX CHILDREN, A CRUMBLING MARRIAGE, THE STOMACH FLU AND IS HOLD-ING DOWN TWO JOBS.

I LOVE A COMPANY WITH A SENSE OF COMPETITION.
PINKLEY

IF I TAKE YOU TO A KENNEL WHEN I GO ON MY BUSINESS TRIP, YOU'LL SIT IN A TINY, LONELY CELL. IT WILL BE HORRIBLE, ELECTRA.

IF I TAKE YOU TO MY MOTHER'S, SHE'LL FIND OUT YOU'RE NOT EN-TIRELY HOUSEBROKEN YET AND WILL LAUNCH INTO A SERIES OF LECTURES AND SPEECHES FROM WHICH I'LL NEVER ESCAPE.

ANY WAY YOU LOOK AT IT, ONE OF US IS GOING TO WIND UP IN A CAGE.

OF COURSE GRANDMA WILL TAKE CARE OF THE BABY WHILE MOMMY GOES AWAY!
MOM, HER NAME IS ELECTRA. SHE'S NOT YOUR GRAND-CHILD.

WON'T IT BE FUN TO STAY AT GRANDMA'S HOUSE??
SHE IS A PUPPY! I WILL NOT HAVE YOU UNDOING FOUR MONTHS OF TRAINING BY TREATING HER LIKE A HUMAN!

HOOCHIE COOCHIE COO...
MOTHER.

SORRY.
FINE. NOW, HERE'S HER BLANKEY, AND SHE LIKES A LITTLE BOWL OF ICE CREAM WHILE SHE WATCHES CAR-TOONS AFTER HER NAP.
ELECTRA

ELECTRA, HOW CAN I LEAVE ?? YOU'RE JUST A BABY !!
SHE'S NOT A BABY ANY-MORE. SHE'LL BE FINE, CATHY.

SHE'LL WON-DER WHERE I AM ! SHE'LL BE SO LONELY !
OH, FOR HEAV-EN'S SAKE. SHE HAS EVERY-THING SHE NEEDS. SHE'LL BE JUST FINE.

I GUESS YOU'RE RIGHT, MOM. THANKS.
ENJOY YOUR BUSINESS TRIP, DEAR.

HOW CAN SHE LEAVE ? SHE'S JUST A BABY !!

IT WOULD DO YOU NO GOOD TO LEAVE ANYWAY, AS THE PAY PHONES ARE ALL BROKEN, THE WASHROOMS ARE ALL BEING CLEANED, THE GIFT SHOPS ARE ALL UNDER CONSTRUCTION, AND THE SNACK BARS ARE ALL BEING PICKETED.

I HATE BEING SQUASHED IN THE MIDDLE SEAT. WILL YOU TRADE WITH ME?
I COULD.

HOWEVER, I'LL BE GETTING UP AT LEAST FOUR TIMES TO PUT MY CONTACTS IN AND OUT.

I'LL GET UP TWICE TO FIX MY HAIR, THREE TIMES TO REDO MY MAKEUP, AND AT LEAST FIVE MORE TIMES BEFORE, DURING AND AFTER DINNER JUST ON GENERAL PRINCIPLE.

NEVER MIND.
NEVER UNDERESTI-MATE THE CLOUT OF TRAVELING WITH SIX LADIES' ROOMS.

I RESERVED A CAR TWO DAYS AGO. THE PAPER-WORK SHOULD BE ALL READY.
WE HAVE NO RECORD OF YOU.
CAR RENTAL

I SPECIFICALLY ASKED FOR A SUBCOMPACT.
ALL WE HAVE IS A FIVE-DOOR STATION WAGON.
CAR RENTAL

I WAS QUOTED $26 A DAY !!
$55 A DAY. STA-TION WAGON, AND IT'LL TAKE AN HOUR TO WRITE UP!

FINE. BUT I'M GOING TO GLARE AT YOU THE WHOLE TIME !!
IT'S ALMOST IMPOSSIBLE TO LOSE A CUSTOM-ER WHO'S GET-TING 500 BONUS POINTS.

I'M BETWEEN MEETINGS, MOM. I WANTED TO SEE IF ELECTRA'S OK.
PERFECT! I LEFT MY SHOES OUT ALL NIGHT AND SHE DIDN'T TOUCH THEM. HERE. I'LL PUT HER ON.

HI, ELECTRA! YOU DIDN'T EAT GRANDMA'S SHOES! WHAT A GOOD GIRL! WHAT A SMART BABY! TELL GRANDMA TO GIVE YOU A NICE BIG BONE!

MOTHERHOOD: FOR EVERY MOMENT OF PRIDE, AN HOUR OF EMBARRASSMENT.

YOU CAN'T FLY ALL THIS WAY AND NOT HAVE DESSERT, CATHY!
OH, NO. NO DESSERT, THANKS.

OUR CITY'S FAMOUS FOR DESSERTS!
I ALREADY HAD YOUR FAMOUS BREAKFAST BUFFET... FOUR-HOUR LUNCH...COCKTAIL HOUR AND FIVE-COURSE DINNER.

WE'RE ALL HAVING DESSERT!
YOU GO AHEAD. I'LL JUST RUN UP TO MY ROOM AND MAKE SOME CALLS SO I'LL BE READY FOR OUR MEETINGS TOMORROW.

HELLO, MOM? PLEASE FEDERAL EXPRESS MY BIGGER SKIRT.

"GET TRAVELER'S CHECKS INSTANTLY, 24 HOURS A DAY, AT ANY OF OUR 36,000 LOCATIONS."
SORRY. YOU HAVEN'T PRE-REGISTERED FOR YOUR P.I.N. NUMBER.

"GET CASH INSTANTLY ON YOUR CHARGE CARD AT ANY OF OUR 75,000 LOCATIONS."
SORRY. THIS MACHINE IS TEMPORARILY OUT OF FUNDS.
CASH

"GET CASH INSTANTLY WITH YOUR BANK ATM CARD AT 98,000 LOCATIONS WORLDWIDE."
SORRY. YOUR CARD ISN'T CODED FOR THIS MACHINE.

I HAVE ENOUGH OF A CREDIT LINE TO BUY A CAR, BUT I CAN'T GET $10 TO CALL A CAB.
UNIVERSAL ATM
AIRPORT

I HAD TO GET A 6 A.M. FLIGHT, SKIP BREAKFAST AND PAY $45 FOR A CAB.... BUT IT'S WORTH IT TO GET BACK TO MY LITTLE PUPPY SOONER...
TAXI

I WOULD HAVE CRAWLED ON MY HANDS AND KNEES TO SEE MY PRECIOUS BABY!! MY ELECTRA! I'M HOME! LEAP INTO MY ARMS!! MOMMY IS HOME!

CHOMP
CHOMP
CHOMP
PUPPY TREATS

THINK BACK TO THE DAYS WHEN YOU HAD TO FINISH WATCHING "BULLWINKLE" RE-RUNS BEFORE YOU'D SAY HELLO TO YOUR MOTHER.
CHOMP
CHOMP
CHOMP
CHOMP
PUPPY TREATS

IF YOU BRUSH ELECTRA'S HAIR FOR TWO MINUTES EACH MORNING, SHE'LL BE EASIER TO GROOM HER WHOLE LIFE.
I KNOW, MOM.

IF YOU SAY ONE FIRM "NO," IT WILL BE 10 TIMES MORE EFFECTIVE THAN 10 TENTATIVE "NOs."
I KNOW, MOM.

IF YOU TAKE ELECTRA OUT AT EXACTLY THE SAME TIME EACH...
I KNOW, MOM!! ENOUGH!! I'VE HEARD ENOUGH!!

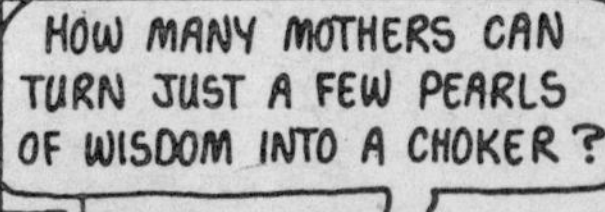
HOW MANY MOTHERS CAN TURN JUST A FEW PEARLS OF WISDOM INTO A CHOKER?

ELECTRA

ELECTRA WAS PERFECT WHILE I WAS GONE, MOM ??
OF COURSE SHE WAS PERFECT!
ELECTRA

SHE...UM... DIDN'T HAVE ANY ACCI-DENTS ??
CERTAINLY NOT. SET CLEAR RULES FOR YOUNG ONES, AND THEY WILL ALWAYS FOLLOW THEM!

WHEN YOU'VE BEEN A PARENT AS LONG AS I HAVE, YOU'LL KNOW THE IMPORTANCE OF ESTABLISHING WHO'S BOSS!!

NOW MAY I CALL THE CARPET FU-MIGATOR ??
GIVE HER A SECOND TO BACK OUT OF THE DRIVEWAY.

YOU'RE GOING HOME ON TIME FOR ONCE, CATHY ?
I HAVE TO GET OUT OF HERE, CHARLENE.
CHARLENE

ALL I'VE DONE FOR TWO WEEKS IS WORK... BUSINESS TRIPS... BUSINESS MEALS... DEADLINES... REPORTS... POWER BATTLES... EMERGENCIES...
CHARLENE

FOR ONCE I HAVE TO JUST GO HOME AND GET BACK IN TOUCH WITH MY GENTLE, FEMININE SIDE...

....THE HOUSE CLEANER.

HOW ARE YOU DOING, CATHY ?
OH, IRVING, MY PLANE TRIP TO MY MEETING WAS A NIGHTMARE!!

THAT WAS FIVE DAYS AGO. YOU MADE IT.
THE FIRST DAY OF MEETINGS WAS HORRIBLE!

THAT'S ALL OVER NOW. IT'S HISTORY. HOW ARE YOU TODAY ?
FINE. TODAY I'M JUST FINE.

SOMETIMES I FEEL LIKE A NEWSPAPER THAT GOT THROWN OUT BEFORE ANYONE READ IT.

WASHINGTON SOURCES HAVE ANNOUNCED THAT, IN THE EVENT OF A NUCLEAR ATTACK, IRS AGENTS ARE EXPECTED TO RESUME COLLECTING TAXES WITHIN 30 DAYS.

NO ONE KNOWS HOW AN AGENCY THAT STILL CAN'T GET ITS "QUESTION HOTLINE" TO WORK HAS BEEN ABLE TO CREATE A PLAN FOR COLLECTING YOUR TAXES AFTER YOUR CITY'S BEEN NUKED...

...HOWEVER, ONE THING REMAINS FAIRLY CLEAR....

CROSS "HAD A STOMACHACHE" OFF MY LIST OF EXCUSES FOR NOT FILING THIS YEAR.

I MADE $12,216 IN HOUSE PAYMENTS LAST YEAR, AND REDUCED THE AMOUNT I OWE BY $1,300.

I MADE $3,241 IN CAR PAYMENTS, AND STILL OWE $6,700 ON A CAR THAT RUNS ONLY TWO DAYS A WEEK.

I WORKED HARDER THAN I'VE EVER WORKED IN MY LIFE, WAS MORE CAREFUL ABOUT WHAT I SPENT, AND ENDED THE YEAR $85,400 IN THE HOLE.

AS LONG AS I'M SINKING INTO THE MUCK, I MIGHT AS WELL BE WEARING A NICE NEW PAIR OF SHOES.
SHOES

I CAN'T STAND PAYING TAXES IF I THINK THE GOVERNMENT ISN'T USING MY MONEY CAREFULLY.
REST ASSURED, CATHY...
ACCOUNTANT

ALL THE MONEY YOU SWEATED AND SLAVED FOR THIS YEAR WENT TO HELP FINANCE THE IRS' $1.9 MILLION STUDY OF HOW LONG IT TAKES PEOPLE TO FILL OUT TAX FORMS.

IN FACT, ALL THE MONEY YOU WILL EVER MAKE IN YOUR LIFE WILL GO TOWARD PAYING OFF THE RESEARCH TEAM WHO SPENT FIVE YEARS DETERMINING THAT IT WILL TAKE YOU 24 MINUTES TO READ THE INSTRUCTIONS ON FORM 1040 EZ!


...EXCEPT, OF COURSE, THE $150 YOU'LL BE PAYING ME TO EXPLAIN THE INSTRUCTIONS.

ACCOUNTANT

DO YOU REALIZE WHAT A TAX BREAK YOU'D GET IF YOU WERE MARRIED, CATHY?
THAT ISN'T TRUE ANYMORE, MOM.
MISC. RECPTS.

OF COURSE IT IS! IF YOU WERE MARRIED...
FINE. SAY I GOT MARRIED. THEN WOULD YOU STOP?! THEN COULD WE NOT HAVE THIS CONVERSATION EVERY YEAR?!

THEN COULD WE TALK ABOUT SOMETHING ELSE FOR ONCE??!

DO YOU REALIZE WHAT A TAX BREAK YOU'D GET IF YOU HAD CHILDREN?
MISC. RECPTS.

JAN. 19, 1988:
ORDERED $49 OF TAKEOUT FOOD BECAUSE I DIDN'T WANT THE CASHIER TO THINK I WAS EATING DINNER ALONE.
1988 EXPENSES

MAY 3, 1988:
SPENT $76 ON GOURMET DESSERTS FOR A DINNER PARTY. ATE THEM MYSELF BEFORE THE GUESTS ARRIVED.
1988 EXPENSES

AUG. 26, 1988:
ATE $103 OF FROZEN FOOD BECAUSE THE POWER WENT OFF FOR 10 MINUTES AND I DIDN'T WANT IT ALL TO MELT AND GO TO WASTE.

THEY TOLD ME TO BUILD A NEST EGG, BUT NO ONE MENTIONED I WASN'T SUPPOSED TO EAT IT.
Guisewite

MY TAXES ARE PAID, AND MY NEW FINANCIAL ORGANIZER IS IN MY PURSE.
U.S. MAIL

FROM THIS MOMENT ON, EVERY DIME WILL BE RECORDED, EVERY TRANSACTION DOCUMENTED, EVERY RECEIPT NOTARIZED, INDEXED AND FILED!

U.S. MAIL

THE ONE DAY OF THE YEAR I'M FULLY PREPARED TO KEEP TRACK OF MY MONEY, I HAVE NOTHING LEFT TO SPEND.
U.S. MAIL

ARE YOU SURE YOU CAN CANCEL YOUR PLANS WITH ANDREA, CATHY?
SURE, IRVING. IT'S THE FIRST RULE OF WOMANHOOD: IF A MAN CALLS, THE WOMAN FRIEND IS DUMPED!

HELLO, ANDREA?
OH, CATHY! IT TOOK ALL DAY, BUT I HAVE A SITTER LINED UP FOR 7 TO 7:45, AND ANOTHER STARTING AT 7:30...

MY HUSBAND SHOULD BE HOME AT 9, UNLESS HE'S RUNNING LATE, IN WHICH CASE I HAVE A BACK-UP ON CALL FROM 9 TO 10:30... ...WHEW! I CAN'T WAIT TO GET OUT OF HERE!

THE SECOND RULE OF WOMANHOOD: A FRIEND CAN BE DUMPED, BUT A MOTHER IS FOREVER.

OUR BABY SITTER CANCELED AT THE LAST MINUTE, DIDN'T SHE, ZENITH? CAN YOU SAY HI TO YOUR AUNT CATHY?

LOOK, ZENITH! A PUPPY!! IT'S CATHY'S NEW PUPPY, ELECTRA! SEE? CAN YOU PAT THE NICE PUPPY? OH, I HAVE TO GET A PICTURE!
Z

EEYAA!
WAIT, HONEY! MOMMY WANTS TO GET A PICTURE! WAIT! MOMMY HAS TO FIX YOUR LITTLE BOW!!

IT'S SO GOOD TO SEE YOU, CATHY!
YOU HAVEN'T EVEN LOOKED AT ME YET.
8

YOUR DOG SNAPPED AT MY BABY!
YOUR BABY WAS YANKING ON MY PUPPY'S TAIL!
SHE KNOCKED HER DOWN ON PURPOSE!
SHE BIT MY PUPPY'S EAR!
WAH!
BARK!

WHY DON'T YOU LOCK THAT MANIAC IN THE KITCHEN?!

...WHAT ARE WE DOING, CATHY?? LOOK! THEY LOVE EACH OTHER...
WE WERE JUST BEING OVERPROTECTIVE...

YOUR MANGY FLEABAG IS SLOBBERING GERMS ON HER FACE!
YOUR LITTLE HOODLUM IS TRYING TO PINCH HER NOSE!!

ZENITH WANTS A SNACK, CATHY. WHERE ARE YOUR CHEERIOS?
I DON'T HAVE ANY CHEERIOS, ANDREA.
DOG FOOD

OH, HA, HA! ALL MY REGULAR FRIENDS ARE MOTHERS! I FORGOT THERE WERE HOMES WITH NO CHEERIOS!!
WELL, EXCUSE ME.

OH, CATHY, I'M SORRY. I JUST FORGOT WHAT A SINGLE PERSON'S KITCHEN IS LIKE.
THAT'S OK, ANDREA. I WAS A LITTLE DEFENSIVE.

WHERE ARE YOUR ORGANIC RICE CAKES?
HERE. LET HER GNAW ON A FROZEN SINGLE SERVING POUCH.

AACK! ZENITH! THAT'S DOG FOOD! YOU DO NOT EAT DOG FOOD!!
"CHOMP CHOMP"
DOG

YOU ARE NOT A DOG! YOU'RE A LITTLE PERSON! A LITTLE BILINGUAL, MUSICALLY GIFTED, 143 IQ PERSON!

WHY DO YOU THINK MOMMY HAS SPENT 24 HOURS A DAY ENRICHING YOUR INCREDIBLE LITTLE MIND WITH THE WHOLE DAZZLING SCOPE OF HUMAN POTENTIAL???

SHE SEEMS TO HAVE MASTERED BELLIGERENCE.
WHERE ARE YOUR BIODE-GRADABLE FACE WIPES?
SPLAT!
"CHOMP CHOMP"

DO YOU THINK YOU'LL EVER HAVE A BABY, CATHY ?
YAP YAP YAP YAP
BAM BAM BAM

I HOPE SO, ANDREA. DO YOU THINK YOU'LL EVER GET A DOG ?
I HOPE SO.
YAP YAP YAP YAP
BAM BAM BAM

THERE'S NOTHING LIKE SEEING SOME-ONE ELSE'S LITTLE ONE TO REAFFIRM THAT OLD FEELING...
YEAH...

MINE WILL BE DIFFERENT....
YAP YAP YAP YAP YAP YAP
BAM BAM BAM BAM BAM

ZENITH DEMANDS ATTENTION EVERY SECOND OF THE DAY, CATHY.
MY JOB IS LIKE THAT, TOO. A CRISIS EVERY SECOND!

SHE NEEDS THIS... WANTS THAT... SHE FUSSES, WHINES, SHRIEKS...
HA, HA! MY JOB IS EXACTLY LIKE THAT!

OH, PLEASE... THERE'S A BIG DIFFERENCE BETWEEN A LITTLE HUMAN BEING AND SOME JOB!

MINE IS NEVER GOING TO GROW UP!!

WHEN YOU SPEND TIME WITH YOUR MARRIED GIRLFRIENDS, YOU GET FIRED UP AND START NAGGING ME ABOUT MAKING A COMMITMENT, CATHY...

WHEN YOU SPEND TIME WITH YOUR SINGLE GIRLFRIENDS, YOU GET FIRED UP AND TRY TO TRICK ME INTO MAKING A COMMITMENT...

ANY TIME YOU GO OUT WITH THE GIRLS, I WIND UP GETTING SOME SPEECH ABOUT COMMITMENT!
THEREFORE, IF YOU WERE WITH ME MORE OF THE TIME, WE WOULDN'T HAVE THESE PROBLEMS, WOULD WE?

AAUGH!!
SORRY. I JUST GOT OFF THE PHONE WITH MY MOTHER.

ELECTRA, YOU'RE SUPPOSED TO BE MY GUARD DOG. WHEN SOMEONE COMES TO THE DOOR, YOU'RE SUPPOSED TO BARK.

YOUR JOB IS TO PROTECT ME, OK. ANY TIME YOU HEAR A NOISE, BARK.

DING DONG!
AACK.

I DIDN'T HEAR ANY BARKING.
SHE SENSED THAT YOU WERE FRIENDLY.

WHEN YOUR FRIENDS HAVE CHILDREN, NOTHING CHANGES BETWEEN YOU, IRVING.

WHEN MY FRIENDS HAVE CHILDREN, THE WHOLE FRIENDSHIP DETERIORATES. WE DON'T EVEN SPEAK THE SAME LANGUAGE ANYMORE!

MEN DON'T KNOW WHAT IT'S LIKE TO BE SO CLOSE TO SOMEONE AND HAVE SOME LITTLE BABY COME BETWEEN THEM, DO THEY, ELECTRA? NO!

N-O-O-O-O...MEN JUST DON'T KNOW, DO THEY, MY SNUGGLY LITTLE CUPCAKE???
MEN GET A HINT NOW AND THEN.

AND WOULD YOU MIND NOT THROWING NEWS-PAPERS ALL OVER MY NICE CLEAN FLOOR ??!
HEY, SORRY! I'LL JUST GO HOME!

CATHY, YOU'VE BEEN SNAPPING AT ME FOR TWO HOURS. YOU MUST NOT WANT ME HERE.
NO... I DON'T WANT YOU TO GO.

WHY ARE YOU TAK-ING IT OUT ON ME?
NO.. YOU'VE BEEN GREAT. I JUST FEEL FAT AND GROUCHY AND DISGUSTED WITH MYSELF.

THE PERSON I'M REALLY SICK OF IN THIS RELATION-SHIP IS THE ONE I CAN'T BREAK UP WITH.

I'VE BEEN A GROUCH, AND NOW IRVING'S ONE, TOO.
TREAT A MAN WITH ANGER, AND HE'LL RE-SPOND WITH ANGER, CATHY.

TREAT A MAN WITH UNFEELING ALOOFNESS, AND HE'LL RESPOND WITH UNFEELING ALOOFNESS.

BUT TREAT A MAN WITH OPEN, LOVING WARMTH, SEN-SITIVITY, CARING, AND COM-PLETE, UTTER DEVOTION...

...AND HE'LL RUN FOR THE NEAREST PLANE OUT OF TOWN.
THEY ALWAYS SAVE ONE AREA TO EXPRESS THEIR INDI-VIDUALITY.

HI, SWEETIE. ARE YOU STILL PLANNING ON LUNCH THIS SUNDAY?
OF COURSE I'M PLANNING ON LUNCH, MOM!

IF YOU'RE TOO BUSY, I UNDERSTAND.
I'M NOT TOO BUSY.
WE COULD DO IT ANOTHER DAY IF YOU'RE BUSY.
I'M NOT BUSY.
WE COULD TALK ABOUT IT LATER IF YOU'RE BUSY RIGHT NOW.
I AM NOT BUSY NOW.
WE COULD JUST SKIP IT.

MOM, I AM PLANNING ON HAVING LUNCH ON SUNDAY. I AM LOOKING FORWARD TO LUNCH ON SUNDAY!

I WANTED TO GET THE MOTHER'S DAY FESTIVITIES OFF TO AN EARLY START THIS YEAR.

HOW WAS YOUR MOTHER'S DAY LUNCH, CATHY?
GREAT UNTIL MOM WHIPPED OUT HER VIDEO OF FLO NEKERVIS' GRANDCHILDREN.

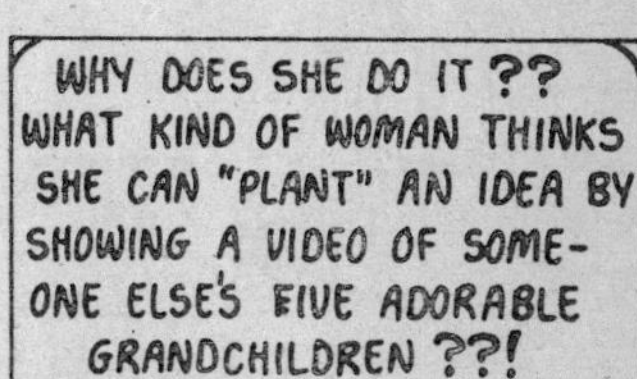
WHY DOES SHE DO IT?? WHAT KIND OF WOMAN THINKS SHE CAN "PLANT" AN IDEA BY SHOWING A VIDEO OF SOMEONE ELSE'S FIVE ADORABLE GRANDCHILDREN??!

...JUST WATCH A COUPLE MINUTES OF IT IRVING. AHEM... ...I JUST WANT YOU TO SEE WHAT I HAVE TO PUT UP WITH.

FOUR POUNDS?? I LOST FOUR POUNDS!!

ELECTRA, I LOST FOUR POUNDS! OH, I'M SO HAPPY! LIFE IS SO WONDERFUL! YOU'RE WONDERFUL!

WHAT A BEAUTIFUL PUPPY!! I LOVE MY BEAUTIFUL PUPPY! LET'S FIND YOU A TOY! LET'S FIX YOU A SNACK! LIFE IS GRAND!! I LOST FOUR POUNDS!!

ATTENTION, DOGS OF THE WORLD: TO IMPROVE YOUR QUALITY OF LIFE, PUT YOUR NOSE ON THE DIAL OF THE SCALE AND SHOVE TO THE RIGHT ONE INCH.

IF I GET INVITED TO A MOONLIGHT BARBECUE IN JUNE, THIS WOULD BE PERFECT...

IF THE HANDSOME MAN I MEET AT THE BARBECUE TAKES ME DANCING EVERY NIGHT AND I LOSE 15 POUNDS BY THE FOURTH OF JULY, THIS WOULD BE ADORABLE...

IF WE SPEND AUGUST HORSE-BACK RIDING IN THE FRENCH COUNTRYSIDE AND STOP FOR ESPRESSO AT A LITTLE CAFÉ, THIS WOULD BE DARLING TO TOSS OVER MY SHOULDERS AS THE SUN SETS AND THE MEDITERRANEAN BREEZE COOLS THE SULTRY RIVIERA AIR...

THIS WOULD BE CUTE TO WEAR TO THE GROCERY STORE.
GET REAL, MOM.

YAWN... ANOTHER HOUR UNTIL MY BREAK... I'M BORED TO DEATH...
ME, TOO... ...YAWN... WHERE'D YOU PUT THAT LAST CUSTOMER?
1
SWIMWEAR

ROOM #1... SHE'S PROBABLY JUST STUFFING HERSELF INTO THE FIRST BATHING SUIT...
HO, HUM... ... SHE COULD BE IN THERE ALL DAY...
CLICK!

AAACK!!
1
RIP
RIP
WAD
RIP

NOTHING LIGHTS UP A ROOM LIKE A NICE NEW FLUORESCENT BULB.

IF YOUR CHEST IS A LITTLE SMALL, THIS SWIMSUIT WILL SQUASH IT COMPLETELY FLAT...

IF YOUR STOMACH'S TOO BIG, THIS WILL SPREAD OUT LIKE GIANT NEON ARROWS POINTING AT THE FLAB... THIGHS TOO PLUMP? THIS ONE SQUISHES THEM INTO TWO BIG BULGES, ABOVE AND BELOW THE LEG LINE.

NO MATTER WHAT YOUR FIGURE PROBLEM, WE HAVE A SUIT THAT WILL MAKE IT WORSE!

YOU'RE TRYING THEM ON??
CURIOSITY TAKES OVER WHERE HOPE LEAVES OFF.

NO NEED. OUR DRESSING ROOM MONITORS HAVE THE WHOLE THING ON VIDEOTAPE.

HOW ABOUT THIS ONE WITH THE NICE RUF- FLED SKIRT?
NO. A RUFFLED SKIRT MEANS YOU'RE TRYING TO HIDE YOUR REAR.

YOU ARE TRYING TO HIDE YOUR REAR.
I WANT A SUIT THAT HIDES MY REAR WITHOUT AN- NOUNCING TO THE WORLD THAT I'M HIDING MY REAR!

FOR ONCE IN MY LIFE, I WANT A BATHING SUIT THAT DOESN'T RELY ON SOME OBVIOUS GIMMICK!

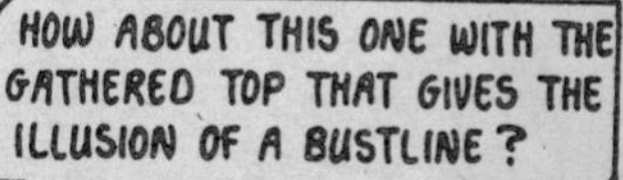

HOW ABOUT THIS ONE WITH THE GATHERED TOP THAT GIVES THE ILLUSION OF A BUSTLINE?
OK.

CAN YOU BEND OVER IN THE BATHING SUIT WITHOUT REVEALING ANYTHING YOU DON'T WANT REVEALED?
YES!

CAN YOU SIT AND THEN STAND UP WITHOUT HAVING TO TUG AT FIVE DIFFERENT AREAS OF THE SUIT?
YES!

CAN YOU LOOK AT THE BACK OF THE SUIT WITHOUT...
THUNK!

STRANGE HOW LIFE'S BIGGEST OBSTACLES ALWAYS SNEAK UP FROM BEHIND.

IF MEN HAD TO GO THROUGH A FRACTION OF WHAT WOMEN DO TO BUY A BATHING SUIT, THE POOLS AND BEACHES OF THE WORLD WOULD SHUT DOWN COMPLETELY !!

THAT'S NOT TRUE, CATHY. MEN HAVE THE SAME TROUBLE.
YOU DO ??
WE HATE SEEING OURSELVES IN SWIMSUITS AFTER BEING INSIDE ALL WINTER.
REALLY ??

IT'S EXACTLY THE SAME HORRIBLE PROBLEM FOR MEN AS IT IS FOR WOMEN.
OH, IRVING, YOU MAKE ME FEEL SO MUCH BETTER....

...SO AS LONG AS YOU'LL BE AT THE MALL ANYWAY, WOULD YOU JUST PICK UP A SUIT FOR ME ? BOXER STYLE, 34" WAIST.

SWIMSUIT NO. 1: DOESN'T FIT. WOMAN BLAMES HERSELF. HANGS IT NEATLY BACK ON ITS LITTLE HANGER.

SWIMSUIT NO. 2: DOESN'T FIT. WOMAN PARTIALLY BLAMES HERSELF. PARTIALLY HANGS IT BACK ON ITS LITTLE HANGER.

SWIMSUITS NOS. 3-50: DON'T FIT.
YOU DISGUST ME! YOU REPULSE ME! NO ONE COULD FIT INTO YOU, YOU OVER-PRICED IMPORTS! HAH!
STOMP STOMP
STOMP STOMP

JUST ONCE I WISH THE HUMAN SPIRIT WOULD TRIUMPH IN SOMEONE ELSE'S DEPARTMENT.

THAT DOES IT. I'M BOYCOTT-ING SWIM-SUITS THIS YEAR, MOM.
YOU BOY-COTTED SWIM-SUITS LAST YEAR, CATHY.
SWIMWEAR

LOOK WHO'S TALKING. YOU HAVEN'T BOUGHT A NEW SWIMSUIT SINCE 1956.
HA, HA! I GUESS IT RUNS IN THE FAMILY!
SWIMWEAR

WHAT RUNS IN THE FAMILY?
AS OUR FIGURES MATURE, WE KNOW THAT GOOD OLD COVERAGE IS MORE IMPORTANT THAN SOME FLASHY TREND!

WHAT HAVEN'T I TRIED ON YET??
NOTHING BRINGS THEM AROUND LIKE A FEW MIN-UTES WITH MOM.

MY LEGS LOOK FAT.
MY WAIST LOOKS FAT.
MY ARMS LOOK FAT.

MY KNEES LOOK FAT.
MY ANKLES LOOK FAT.
MY CHIN LOOKS FAT.
MY HAIR LOOKS FAT.
MY EYELIDS LOOK FAT.
MY FEET LOOK FAT.
MY TEETH LOOK FAT.
MY FINGERS LOOK FAT.

INCREDIBLE.

THE ONLY CELL IN MY BODY THAT ISN'T BUSY LOOKING FAT IS THINKING ABOUT WHAT I CAN EAT FOR LUNCH.

$75 FOR THIS SWIMSUIT ?! ARE YOU CRAZY ? ARE YOU OUT OF YOUR MIND ??
SWIM

EVERY YEAR THE SUITS GET SMALLER AND THE PRICES GET LARGER ... AND THE WOMEN OF THIS COUNTRY ARE SICK OF IT !!

WE ARE NOT GOING TO TAKE IT ANYMORE ! UNDERSTAND ?? WE ARE NOT GOING TO TAKE IT !

DIDN'T FIT ?
ARE YOU KIDDING ? IF IT HAD FIT, I WOULD HAVE GIVEN HER $300 FOR IT.

WE DO NOT BELIEVE A WOMAN'S WORTH IS MEASURED BY THE SHAPE OF HER BODY!
WE HATE SEXISM! WE HATE LECHERY!
SWIMWEAR

WE DO NOT BUY SWIMSUITS SO WE CAN "GO ON DISPLAY"!
WE COULD GRAB ANY SUIT! IT DOES NOT MATTER!!
SWIMWEAR

WE HAVE EVOLVED TO A WHOLE NEW CONSCIOUSNESS!!
SWIMWEAR

... IF I'M GOING TO BE A HYPOCRITE, AT LEAST I WANT TO LOOK CUTE.
WHERE ARE THE ONES WITH THE LITTLE ZIPPERS UP THE FRONT?
SWIMWEAR

DON'T YOU WANT TO GO TO THE POOL AND TRY OUT YOUR NEW BATHING SUIT, CATHY?
I CAN'T. I HAVE A HEADACHE.

I HAVE A STOMACHACHE.
I HAVE TO WORK.
I HAVE TO DO ERRANDS.
I HAVE TO DO THE LAUNDRY.
I HAVE TO WASH THE CAR.
I HAVE TO CLEAN HOUSE.
I HAVE TO BATHE ELECTRA.
I HAVE TO CALL MY MOTHER.
I HAVE TO BUY GROCERIES.
I HAVE TO PAY BILLS.

ELEVEN LIES IS AS CLOSE TO THE MOMENT OF TRUTH AS I CAN GET FOR THE DAY.

BAD GIRL, ELECTRA! YOU CHEWED UP MY MAIL AGAIN! BAD! BAD! BAD!

...IT'S AN ENGAGEMENT ANNOUNCEMENT FROM JANE! JANE'S ONLY KNOWN HIM FOR SIX MONTHS! HOW CAN JANE BE ENGAGED??!

BLEAH!
RIP
RIP
RIP
RIP
RIP
RIP
RIP
RIP
RIP

HUMANS: YOU CAN'T LIVE WITH THEM, YOU CAN'T LIVE WITHOUT THEM.

HOW DID HE PROPOSE, JANE?
OH, IT WAS SO ROMANTIC!

I DROPPED HINTS FOR MONTHS... I BEGGED, WHINED, WHIMPERED, COAXED, SEDUCED, PLOTTED AND SCHEMED....

THEN, FOR MY GRAND FINALE, I STOMPED OUT OF HIS HOUSE SOBBING THAT I NEVER WANTED TO SEE HIS MISERABLE FACE AGAIN.... AND HE SAID, WELL, OK, MAYBE WE COULD TRY GETTING ENGAGED!!

VERY ROMANTIC.
TECHNICALLY, THE WORDS CAME OUT OF HIS LIPS.
JUST LIKE IN THE MOVIES!

I WOULD NEVER TRICK A MAN INTO WANTING TO BE WITH ME, CHARLENE.
EXCEPT FOR MAKEUP. IT'S OK TO TRICK HIM A LITTLE BIT WITH MAKEUP.
Flowers

AND CLOTHES. TRICKING HIM WITH CLOTHES IS OK.
ALSO COLOGNE, CANDLELIGHT, ROMANTIC MUSIC, SEXY MOVIES AND ALL HIS FAVORITE FOODS.

IT'S OK TO GET HIM EMOTIONALLY DEPENDENT ON ME FOR ALL THE COZY COMFORTS OF LIFE WHILE SIMULTANEOUSLY LETTING HIM HEAR AN OCCASIONAL PHONY MESSAGE ON MY MACHINE FROM ANOTHER MAN... BUT I WOULD NEVER REALLY TRICK HIM!

SOME WOMEN HAVE NO SELF-RESPECT.
WHAT DO YOU THINK THEY'VE TRIED THAT WE HAVEN'T THOUGHT OF YET?...
Flowers

DEEP DOWN, MEN WANT WOMEN TO TAKE CHARGE OF THEIR LOVE LIVES FOR THEM, CATHY.
YOU'RE WRONG, JANE.

MEN LIKE THE WOMAN TO CALL. THEY WANT THE WOMAN TO ASK THEM OUT.
YOU ARE ABSOLUTELY WRONG!

LOTS OF MEN ARE OUT THERE HOPING THE WOMAN WILL PROPOSE TO THEM!
REALLY? YOU THINK SO???

I NEVER TAKE AN IDEA SERIOUSLY UNTIL IT'S BIG ENOUGH TO REALLY HUMILIATE MYSELF WITH.

I'M GOING TO PROPOSE TO IRVING, CHARLENE.
YES! BRAVO! GO FOR IT, CATHY!!

I'LL HELP YOU PLAN WHAT TO SAY! I'LL HELP YOU DECIDE WHAT TO WEAR! I'LL BE THERE FOR YOU 24 HOURS A DAY!! I'M SO PROUD OF YOU! I'M SO HAPPY FOR YOU!!

BUT IF YOU GET MAR-RIED, I'LL KILL YOU! I'LL NEVER FORGIVE YOU! IF YOU DESERT ME FOR A HUSBAND, I'LL NEVER SPEAK TO YOU AGAIN!!!!

I LOVE THE CLEAR MESSAGES I GET FROM MY WOMEN FRIENDS.

THIS SAYS 95% OF ALL MARRIAGES HAPPEN BECAUSE THE WOMAN EITHER PROPOSES HERSELF OR LEADS THE MAN RIGHT TO THE EDGE.
LET ME SEE.
COSMO

YOU'RE SUPPOSED TO PROPOSE TO IRVING, CATHY!
I'M SUPPOSED TO PROPOSE!
COSMO

CLEAN THE HOUSE!
GET SOME GROCERIES!
COOK SOME SNACKS!
PLANT FLOWERS!
BUY NEW CLOTHES!
GET A MAKEOVER!
WASH THE CAR!
CLEAN THE CLOSETS!
LOSE 15 POUNDS!

AFTER $20 BILLION OF RESEARCH, NUCLEAR FUSION HAS JUST BEEN CREATED BY TWO WOMEN AND A COPY OF COSMOPOLITAN MAGAZINE.

I INVITED IRVING TO DINNER IN THE MOST EXPENSIVE RESTAURANT IN TOWN SO I COULD PROPOSE...JUST LIKE YOU SUGGESTED!
YOU'RE KIDDING. YOU'RE GOING THROUGH WITH IT?!

YOU TOLD ME THAT, DEEP DOWN, HE WANTED ME TO PROPOSE... THAT WE BOTH NEEDED THE EMOTIONAL LIBERATION OF A PROPOSAL!!
I DIDN'T THINK YOU'D ACTUALLY DO IT!

CHARLENE, YOU SPENT FIVE HOURS TALKING ME INTO THIS!! THE WHEELS ARE IN MOTION!!!
HA, HA! WELL, GOOD LUCK! WANT A FROZEN YOGURT OR SOMETHING?

NEVER UNDERESTIMATE THE HIGH PRICE OF A CHEAP THERAPIST.

THIS IS THE NIGHT I PROPOSE TO IRVING. MY SWEETIE. THE LOVE OF MY LIFE.

ISN'T THAT CUTE? HE'S DOING THAT FUNNY THING WITH HIS DINNER ROLL. THAT FUNNY THING THAT I HATE. HA, HA. NO. NOT HATE. I ADORE HIS FUNNY LITTLE REPULSIVE HABITS.

NOW HE'S PICKING ALL THE TOMATOES OUT OF HIS SALAD. I HATE WHEN HE PICKS TOMATOES OUT OF HIS SALAD. NO. HE'S MY SWEETIE. I LOVE EVERYTHING HE DOES. EXCEPT THAT. EXCEPT WHEN HE CLINKS HIS SPOON LIKE THAT. NO. CLINKING IS FINE. SO WHAT IF I HAVE TO LISTEN TO THAT CLINKING SPOON FOR THE WHOLE REST OF MY–

JUST ONCE I WISH THEY'D HAVE THEIR REVELATIONS AFTER I GOT MY TIP.

DO WE HAVE TO LISTEN TO THIS MUSIC, IRVING ?
WE ALWAYS LISTEN TO THIS MUSIC, CATHY.

WE ALWAYS LISTEN TO THIS MUSIC BECAUSE YOU ALWAYS PLAY THIS MUSIC.
IF YOU DON'T LIKE THIS MUSIC, WHY DON'T YOU PLAY DIFFERENT MUSIC ?

BECAUSE I'D RATHER LISTEN TO MUSIC I HATE AND KNOW YOU'RE HAPPY THAN LISTEN TO MUSIC I LOVE AND THINK YOU MIGHT NOT LIKE IT. FOR ONCE YOU COULD APPRECIATE THAT AND CHANGE THE TAPE ON YOUR OWN !!

WHY DO I ALWAYS WIND UP GETTING PUNISHED FOR THE NICE THINGS SHE DOES FOR ME ?

FROM THE SECOND I DECIDED TO ASK IRVING TO MARRY ME, I HAVEN'T BEEN ABLE TO STAND BEING IN THE SAME ROOM WITH HIM.

EVERYTHING ABOUT HIM ANNOYS ME. I DON'T LIKE HIS HAIR. I CAN'T STAND HIS CLOTHES. HIS STORIES GIVE ME A HEADACHE AND HIS LAUGH MAKES MY SKIN ITCH.

CATHY, RELAX. YOU HAVE SOMETHING RIGHT NOW WITH IRVING THAT PEOPLE SPEND THEIR WHOLE LIVES SEARCHING FOR...

PERSPECTIVE.
AACK! NOT THAT!!
LEAVE IT TO A MARRIED WOMAN TO TAKE THE ROMANCE OUT OF DISILLUSIONMENT.

IRVING'S ALWAYS PUT HIS OWN INTERESTS AND SCHEDULE BEFORE YOURS, CATHY.
I THOUGHT HE WAS JUST GIVING ME SPACE.

HE'S DONE EVERYTHING POSSIBLE TO AVOID ANY BIG COMMITMENT.
I THOUGHT HE WAS JUST BEING COY.

HE'S BEHAVED EXACTLY THE SAME SINCE THE DAY YOU MET... WHAT GROUNDS DO YOU HAVE TO CRITICIZE HIM NOW?

YOU AREN'T THE PERSON I WAS PRETENDING YOU WERE!!

WHEN SOMETHING WONDERFUL HAPPENS WITH IRVING, SHE RUNS TO TELL HER MOTHER.

WHEN SOMETHING HORRIBLE HAPPENS, SHE RUNS TO TELL HER MOTHER.

THE WHOLE REST OF THE TIME--INCLUDING ALL MOMENTS LEADING UP TO THE WONDERFUL OR HORRIBLE EVENTS--SHE DOESN'T SAY A PEEP.

MOTHERHOOD: ALL HEADLINES, NO TEXT.

I DON'T THINK WE SHOULD SEE EACH OTHER ANYMORE.

WHAT?? YOU DON'T WANT TO SEE EACH OTHER ANY-MORE?? I THOUGHT YOU WERE TOTALLY HAPPY!

WHEN DID YOU DECIDE WE SHOULDN'T SEE EACH OTH-ER ANYMORE?? I CAN'T BELIEVE IT! WHEN WERE YOU GOING TO SPRING THIS ONE ON ME?!!

AT LAST. PERFECT HARMONY.

I CAN'T BELIEVE I WAS PLANNING TO PROPOSE TO YOU. YOU MAKE ME SICK!
YOU REPULSE ME!

YOU DISGUST ME!
YOU LIVE IN FANTASY LAND!
HAH! I'M THE ONLY LINK TO REALITY THIS RELATIONSHIP EVER HAD!
HAH!

SLAM!

...WHAT WOULD YOUR ANSWER HAVE BEEN?

YOU'RE NEVER SEEING IRVING AGAIN?
NEVER. EXCEPT HE HAS TO GET HIS STUFF FROM MY HOUSE AND I HAVE TO GET MY STUFF FROM HIS HOUSE.

AFTER THAT YOU'RE NEVER SEEING HIM AGAIN?
NEVER. EXCEPT HE HAS TO COME OVER AND FIX THE STEREO HE SMASHED WHEN WE HAD OUR LAST FIGHT.

AFTER THAT?
NEVER. EXCEPT I HAVE TO GIVE HIM RIDES UNTIL HIS CAR GETS BUMPED OUT FROM WHEN I ACCI-DENTALLY THREW HIS GOLF CLUBS AT IT.

YOU'RE A ROCK, CATHY.
NOW THAT WE'VE BROKEN UP, I'M SEEING HIM SEVEN NIGHTS A WEEK.

NO MESSAGES. HOW DO I KNOW IF I MADE IRVING JEALOUS OR NOT IF HE DIDN'T LEAVE A MESSAGE ?

YOU WERE HERE, ELECTRA. DID SOMEONE CALL AND NOT LEAVE A MESSAGE ?? DID SOMEONE HANG UP BEFORE THE BEEP ??

HOW MANY TIMES DID SOME-ONE HANG UP BEFORE THE BEEP ?? DID YOU HEAR HIM BREATHING BEFORE THE HANG UP ?? DID IT SOUND LIKE IRVING ? THINK, ELECTRA !

WHATEVER HAPPENED TO THE GOOD OLD DAYS WHEN ALL A DOG HAD TO DO FOR A COOKIE WAS LEARN TO SIT ?

IF THE BREAKUP WAS ALL HIS IDEA, I'D SCREAM, CRY AND HUMILIATE MYSELF BY WRITING DESPERATE LETTERS BEGGING TO HAVE HIM BACK.

IF THE BREAKUP WAS ALL MY IDEA, I'D STOMP AROUND RECITING HIS FLAWS AND BRIBE FRIENDS TO SPY ON HIM AND TELL ME HOW MISERABLE HE WAS.

THE BREAKUP WAS MUTUAL. NO ONE'S FAULT. BOTH SIDES TOTALLY AGREED.

I'VE BEEN ROBBED OF MY WHOLE REPERTOIRE!

YOU'RE NOT UPSET THAT IRVING AND I BROKE UP?
OH, CATHY, ALL THAT MATTERS IS THAT YOU'RE HAPPY.

I'VE ENJOYED GETTING TO KNOW IRVING OVER THE YEARS... BUT I'M JUST YOUR MOTHER! ONLY YOU KNOW WHAT'S RIGHT FOR YOU!

THANKS, MOM. THAT REALLY HELPS.

I HAVE TO START ALL OVER AGAIN!!

I WILL NOT CALL IRVING.
WE'VE BROKEN UP.
I HAD MY REASONS.
GOOD REASONS.

CONCENTRATE ON THE REASONS.
THINK OF ALL THE BAD TIMES.
FOCUS ON THE HIDEOUS TIMES.
ENUMERATE HIS FLAWS.

VISUALIZE HIM AT HIS WORST. DWELL ON EVERY NEGATIVE PERSONALITY TRAIT. DREDGE UP EACH AND EVERY ICKY ENCOUNTER AND FEEL IT FOR THE FIRST TIME ALL OVER AGAIN....

...ANOTHER WILD AND CRAZY SATURDAY NIGHT, SEARCHING FOR NEW WAYS TO KEEP THE BREAKUP FRESH.

BREAKING UP NOT ONLY FREES US TO BE WITH SOMEONE ELSE, BUT ALSO FREES US TO BECOME SOMEONE ELSE...

WHILE WE ALL FEEL THE SAME POWERFUL URGE TO RENEW WHO WE ARE... OVER THE YEARS, EACH SEX HAS FOUND ITS OWN SPECIAL WAY OF LIVING IT OUT....

MEN DRIVE FLASHY RED SPORTS CARS...

...WOMEN WEAR THEM ON OUR HEADS.

AACK! YOU TURNED MY HAIR ORANGE!!
RED. AND BESIDES, IT'LL TONE DOWN IN A COUPLE OF WEEKS.
SALON

MY HAIR IS BRIGHT ORANGE!
NONSENSE. THE RINSE JUST BROUGHT OUT YOUR NATURAL HIGHLIGHTS!
SALON

JUST MAKE SURE YOU LET IT SET OVERNIGHT.
I'M SUPPOSED TO LET IT SET OVERNIGHT ?

OH, YES! YOU'D HATE TO HAVE SPENT $125 ON THIS BEAUTIFUL COLOR AND THEN RISK WASHING IT OUT THE FIRST DAY!
SALON
SALO

HI, CHARLENE. IT'S CATHY. PLEASE TELL MR. PINKLEY I WON'T BE IN TODAY.
RECEPTIONIST

I'M NOT FEELING WELL. THERE'S A FAMILY EMERGENCY. MY CAR BROKE DOWN AND ELECTRA HAS AN IMPORTANT DOCTOR'S APPOINTMENT.
RECEPTIONIST

WHAT COLOR IS YOUR HAIR ?
RECEPTIONIST

FROM THE CRACKLE IN YOUR VOICE, I'D SAY IT'S BRIGHT ORANGE.
HOW DID YOU KNOW ?

IT SAYS TO TEST A STRAND OF HAIR FIRST.
I'VE DONE THIS A MILLION TIMES, CATHY!
INSTRUCTIONS

IT SAYS NOT TO USE ON HAIR THAT'S ALREADY BEEN COLORED ORANGE.
THEY'RE JUST BEING OVER-PROTECTIVE!
INSTRUCTIONS

TRUST ME! I JUST SLATHER ON SOME TINT... WAIT A WHILE.. POP OFF THE LITTLE CAP AND...

AAACK!
MAY I ASSUME I DON'T LOOK LIKE THE WOMAN ON THE BOX?

I DEMAND TO SEE THE DRUG ADDICT WHO DYED MY HAIR ORANGE !!

I'VE SPENT $400 ON EMERGENCY RE-COLORING TREATMENTS, LEAVING MY HAIR AS DRY AND BRITTLE AS STRAW AND I WANT TO KNOW WHAT YOU'RE GOING TO DO ABOUT IT !!!!!
SALON

HOW ABOUT A NICE "SUMMER BLONDE" RINSE ? ONLY $95.
OK.
SALON

...HOPE: YOU CAN BREAK OFF ALL THE ENDS, BUT YOU CAN'T KILL THE ROOTS.

CATHY, IT'S IRVING. I NEED TO SEE YOU.
COOKIES

I CAN'T SEE YOU ANYMORE, IRVING. I'VE CHANGED.
I KNOW YOU'VE CHANGED... BUT I'VE CHANGED, TOO.

I'VE GOTTEN WORSE.
COOKIES